Our Beginnings

SHARON
STERLING

OXFORD
UNIVERSITY PRESS

OXFORD
UNIVERSITY PRESS

70 Wynford Drive, Don Mills, Ontario M3C 1J9
www.oupcan.com

Oxford New York

Athens   Auckland   Bangkok   Bogotá   Buenos Aires   Calcutta   Cape Town
Chennai   Dar es Salaam   Delhi   Florence   Hong Kong   Istanbul   Karachi
Kuala Lumpur   Madrid   Melbourne   Mexico City   Mumbai   Nairobi   Paris
São Paulo   Singapore   Taipei   Tokyo   Toronto   Warsaw

with associated companies in Berlin   Ibadan

Oxford is a trade mark of Oxford University Press
in the UK and in certain other countries

Published in Canada
By Oxford University Press

Copyright © Oxford University Press Canada 2000

The moral rights of the author have been asserted

Database right Oxford University Press (maker)

First published 2000

Canadian Cataloguing in Publication Data

Sterling, Sharon, 1955–
Our beginnings
(Outlooks)
Includes index.
ISBN 0–19–541431–4

Canada – History – Juvenile literature. I. Title. II. Series.

FC172.S73 1999   971   C99–931322–3
F1026.S73 1999

5 6 7 8 – 03 02 01

This book is printed on permanent (acid-free) paper ∞.

Printed in Canada

Contents

Acknowledgements

A work such as this depends a great deal on the primary research and publications of many groups and individuals. In particular, the author would like to acknowledge the work of the Secwepemc Cultural Education Society and their publications, *The Shuswap Cultural Series* and *We Are the Shuswap; You Are Asked to Witness*, published by the Stó:lō Heritage Trust; Ruth Kirk, *Wisdom of the Elders: Native Traditions on the Northwest Coast*; and Cheryl Coull, *A Traveller's Guide to British Columbia*. Any errors or misinterpretations of these works are, of course, entirely the responsibility of the author.

The author and the publisher wish to thank the following consultants for their guidance and advice:

Sharon Anderson
David Cameron Elementary School
Victoria, BC

Sheila Borman
Kitchener Elementary School
Burnaby, BC

The author and the publisher also extend their thanks to the following people for reviewing the manuscript:

Donna Anderson
Coal Tyee Elementary School
Nanaimo, BC

Judy Dallin
Coordinator of Aboriginal Programs
Langley, BC

Pat Horstead
Maple Ridge Primary School
Maple Ridge, BC

Professor Ian Wright
Faculty of Education
Department of Curriculum Studies
Vancouver, BC

Also thanks to the following people who helped in various ways during the development of the manuscript:

Jennie Heys
Port Coquitlam, BC

Nella Nelson
First Nations Coordinator
Greater Victoria, BC

Tom Sampson and Family
Tsartlip First Nation
Brentwood Bay, BC

Bernice Shadow
First Nations Education
Cultural Coordinator
Peace River North, BC

Colleen Walton
George Jay School
Greater Victoria, BC

Betty Wilson
Brooks Secondary School
Powell River, BC

Credits

Cover Design: Brett Miller

Text Design: Brett Miller/Paul Sneath

Layout & Cartographic Art: Paul Sneath

Illustrations: Heather Graham, Julian Mulock, VISU*TronX*

Cover Image: Eagle Mask by Lyle Wilson. Photo courtesy Inuit Gallery of Vancouver, Ltd.

Introduction

*O*ur *Beginnings* is a **social studies** textbook.

In social studies, you investigate the lives of people—the way they do things, what they believe in, and the tools they use to get things done. You also learn about the natural world. Social studies helps you discover what things were like in the past and what things are like today.

Most of *Our Beginnings* investigates our part of North America in the time before there was a country called Canada. You can learn what life was like then for Aboriginal peoples— the first people to live here. You can also find out about the explorers who came here from Europe and how these two groups got along.

Learning about these *beginnings* can help you understand the way things are for Aboriginal peoples and others today. You can use this information to decide how you think things should be done in the future.

You *can* make a difference. This year in social studies, learn, have fun, and take part in making your school the kind of place you think it should be.

Chapter 1

Getting Along

Getting along means working with others to solve problems and get things done. It also means playing together and having fun!

Think about times when you work or play with friends. Do you ever disagree? If you do, that's normal. In most groups, people agree about some ideas and feelings, but disagree about others. They can still figure out ways to get along, though.

In this chapter, you can learn some things that might help you get along in groups. You can also find out why you should think for yourself when you watch television!

Nice to Meet You!

In order to get along in groups, you have to find out what is special about each person. You also have to find out what ideas and feelings you share.

Individuals and Groups

An **individual** is one person. There are millions of people on earth, but there is no one exactly like you. You have your own special looks and your own way of talking and thinking. Every other person you meet is also a special individual.

An individual can also be part of many different **groups**. Your family, your class, and your community are all groups that you belong to.

Culture

Your **culture** is the way of life followed by your family or community. We all get used to our own cultures. When we meet people of different cultures, we might think, "That's not how we do it in my family!" To get along with others, it helps to respect their cultures.

Reading Hint

When you see a word in **boldface**, pay attention! This is an important word. The explanation of what it means will be nearby on the page or even in the same sentence.

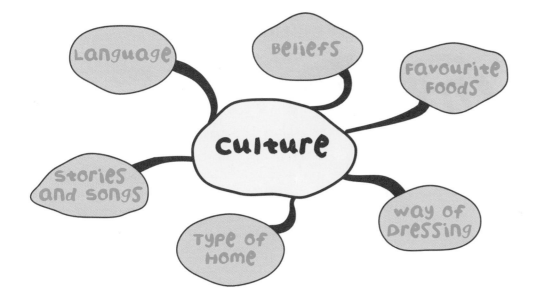

This **web** shows some of the things that make up a culture. A web is one way to show how the parts of something fit together. What do you think is the most interesting part of culture on this web? What would you add?

In The Words Of...

Kids Like You!

On these pages, students your age talk about themselves and their families. Sometimes they talk about **traditions**. A tradition is something that has been done the same way for a long time.

As you read what these students say and look at the pictures, try to find interesting ideas that are new to you. Also look for ways these students are like you and your friends.

My name is Jessica

This is me at school.
I'm signing the sentence "I love you."
Can you tell that I was painting that day?

About Me

I like to play games with my sister. "Snakes and Ladders" and "Scrabble" are two of my favourites. I also like writing to my friends Josh and Kyle in Ontario. Skipping is my favourite outdoor sport.

I was born Deaf. Since I was very small, I have used American Sign Language (ASL) to talk to people.
In ASL, you use your hands to make words and show ideas.
If other people know ASL, I can understand them.
I have lots of friends at school who know ASL.

About My Family

In my family we like to do things together. Sometimes we work together —like cleaning out the garage. Other times we have fun together—like when we go camping every summer. My family is hearing, but they know ASL. This makes it easy for us to get along.

I'm Tashina!

This picture shows me in the gym.
I'm number 9 on the George Jay Junior Girls basketball team.

About Me

I love sports! I play basketball and soccer. I also like art and music. In art, my favourite colours are white, black, blue, and purple. I'd like to do more First Nations art. Once my daddy made some wooden masks and I painted them. Right now my favourite groups are Brandy, The Spice Girls, and 'NSync.

About My Family

I'm Kwakwaka 'wakw. I have about 200 relatives–really!
I have fun with my cousins when we get together for family celebrations such as birthdays and weddings.

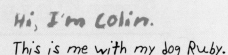

Hi, I'm Colin.

This is me with my dog Ruby.

About Me

I like all kinds of animals. I have a dog called Ruby and a gerbil called Mini. My favourite sports are baseball and football. I play on the Blue Devils football team.

About My Family

I have two favourite family traditions. Every summer my dad and I go on a camping trip. My mom doesn't come because she hates camping! In the summer we also get together with my cousins at Grandma's house in Victoria. It's fun, and we always have a big salmon dinner.

Hello! My Name Is Cleo.

This is me at the library. I like to read fairy tales.

About Me

After school, I like playing soccer with my friends Tristan, Tyler, and Garret. If I'm by myself, I like skipping. Indoors, I like to read or play video games. One of my favourite video games is about a fox who tries to find a hedgehog.

About My Family

My sister and I were born in Canada, but our parents were born in China. At home, we speak Cantonese Chinese. Every day after regular school I go to Chinese school to learn to write Chinese. It takes a lot of practice, but I like it.

In my family we do many things other Canadians do. We also have some special Chinese traditions. One tradition is that we give gifts of money wrapped in red paper for Chinese New Year. This happens in late January or early February.

Try This

You are the topic of this project. Make a poster that tells people what is special about you. Include information about your family traditions.

HOW TO... Start Projects

In social studies, you'll do many different projects. A project gives you a chance to research a topic and present what you find. Sometimes you can choose the topic and the way you want to present the information. Other times your teacher will ask you to do a project in a certain way.

Here are some questions to ask before you begin:

1. What is my topic?
2. Where should I look for information about my topic?
3. How am I going to present my information?
4. What things do I need to include in my project?
5. When do I have to be finished?
6. How can I tell if I've done a good job?

Facts and Opinions

To get along with others you have to share ideas. When you share ideas, it is important to know the difference between **facts** and **opinions**.

A fact is information that you can prove to be true. Here are some facts:

- *All kids in the class brought cookies.*

- *I spent all day playing at Mia's house.*

- *When we watched "George Terrific" we couldn't stop laughing.*

- *We waited for Lionel.*

An opinion is a person's idea about something. It might be an idea about what people should do or about what something is like.

Here are some opinions:

- *We think all kids in the class should bring cookies.*

- *I think Mia is fun to play with.*

- *We think "George Terrific" is the best cartoon on TV.*

- *I think we should wait for Lionel.*

Forming Opinions

People form opinions based on the information they have about a topic.

A **biased opinion** is an unfair opinion based on only a little bit of information. People with biased opinions often repeat what they have heard other people say.

A **fair opinion** is based on collecting **evidence** before deciding what you think. Evidence includes facts and examples that give you information. People who have fair opinions think for themselves before repeating what others say.

To make sure you form fair opinions, keep your eyes and ears open for the facts!

Sources of Information

Stories of the Elders

Elders are older people who have a lot of knowledge and wisdom. The Elders in your community might tell stories about the beliefs, history, and traditions of your culture. Listening to stories

Bias happens when a person judges something or someone without first getting the facts or other information. How could having a biased opinion make it hard to get along with others?

told by the Elders of other communities can help you learn about other cultures.

Interviews
In **interviews** you ask a person questions to get information. The questions might be about the person's life or about something the person knows.

There is a lot of information out there! What sources of information do you see in this picture?

Elders, family members, friends, and other people in your community are all good sources of information about many topics.

Books
Books can tell you many things about people, places, and events all over the world. **Fiction books** tell stories about imaginary people, places, and events. **Non-fiction books** present facts, examples, and opinions about real people, places, and events. Books can tell you about things that are happening today. They can also tell you about things that happened long ago.

Newspapers
Newspaper reports tell you about current events. **Current events** are real events that are happening today. Some newspaper reports are about people and events in your community. Some reports are about people and events in other communities.

The Internet
On the Internet, you can exchange information with people from around the world. You can also read fiction from many cultures and look up facts about people, places, and events.

Information on the Internet comes from **Web sites**. A Web site includes computer pages of

HOW TO... Work in a Group

When you work in a group, it is important for everyone to share their ideas. Here are some things that can help you get along.

1. Give everyone a chance to speak.

2. Listen to what other people have to say. Think about what they mean.

3. Speak up when you have an idea or opinion. Give reasons for what you think.

4. If you disagree with someone, ask for more information. Is there a part of the idea you can agree with?

words and pictures on a particular topic. Anyone who wants to can create a Web site. The person doesn't have to be an expert on a topic or have the information checked by anyone. So be especially careful to check information from a Web site with another source. It might include errors or present a biased opinion.

Television

When you watch television, you see many different people. Some programs present facts about real people and places. These programs are like non-fiction books. Other programs tell stories. These programs are like fiction books. **Comedies** and **dramas** are two kinds of television programs that tell stories. Comedies are funny. Dramas tell serious stories.

Try This

In a group, make a chart that shows what you know about sources of information. List all the sources you can think of.

For each source, record at least one fact and one example. Also give your opinion of how easy it is to use or how useful it is. If you haven't used a source, you might say, "Don't know."

Ask one member of your group to present your chart to the class. You might report that you have different opinions!

Sources of Information	Facts	Examples	Opinions
stories of the Elders			
interviews			

Tuning Out Stereotypes

Here's a question for you:

- *Do you think television helps to spread stereotypes?*

This question asks your opinion. Nobody knows for sure what the answer is. Your job is to make sure you form a fair opinion.

This is a BIG QUESTION. The first step in investigating a question like this is to break it down into SMALL QUESTIONS. Answering small questions gives you the facts and examples you need to answer the big question.

Here are the three small questions we'll answer in this section:

- *What is a stereotype?*

- *Are there stereotypes on television?*

- *Do people believe what they see on television?*

What is a stereotype?

A **stereotype** is a biased or unfair way of showing what a person is like.

In real life, each person is an individual with many different **qualities**. Qualities are likes and dislikes, ways of doing things, and habits that make each person special. A stereotype shows only one or two qualities of a person. These qualities come from a biased opinion of what people from a particular group or culture are like.

The Trouble with Stereotypes

If you believe stereotypes, you never get to know what another person or culture is really like.

Some stereotypes are also unkind. They can make another person feel badly or not welcome. If you repeat these stereotypes and the person you are talking about hears you, it may be hard for you to be friends.

How Stereotypes Spread

Stereotypes spread when people repeat something they have read, seen, or heard without thinking for themselves.

Spotting Stereotypes

To stop stereotypes from spreading, you have to be able to spot them. When you spot a stereotype, don't repeat it.

You might find stereotypes when you talk to people or listen to jokes. You might also find stereotypes when you read books, watch television, or search the Internet. Here are some signs to help you spot a stereotype:

• The person is either too good or too bad. It doesn't seem real to you.

• It makes it seem like all people of one group or culture are the same.

• It makes it seem like one group or culture is better than another.

Are there stereotypes on television?

Yes! Here are some reasons why.

They Are Not Real People

Most of the comedies and dramas we see on television show people in situations that *could* be real.

Remember, though, that these television people are *not* real. They are **characters** invented by a writer.

Stereotypes Make the Writer's Job Easier

Television programs include stereotypes because they make the writer's job easier. Most television programs run for half an hour or an hour. This isn't very much time to explain what a character is like and tell the story.

So, to tell the story quickly, writers often use stereotypes. Usually you have seen these stereotypes before in other television programs. They are **familiar**. When we see something familiar, we can form an opinion about the character in a few seconds. This saves time and keeps the story moving.

Commercials Want to Get Your Attention

Television commercials also use stereotypes. Commercials are even shorter than television programs, so the writer *really* needs to save time! Also, when people see something familiar in a commercial, it makes them more interested in buying the **product**. The product is the thing the commercial is trying to sell.

We all have many different qualities. What are some of yours?

Are you influenced by what you see on television? Ask yourself this question:

- *Have I ever wanted something I saw in a TV commercial?*

What does your answer tell you? Do you think others would give the same answer? Why?

Do people believe what they see on television?

Some people believe what they see on television. Other people think for themselves.

It's not always easy to think for yourself when you watch television. What you see can seem so real and exciting that you might forget you are watching actors. Television commercials are especially good at pretending to show real events.

When something is strong enough to change the way you think or act, it **influences** you. If you watch a lot of television, then it can influence what you think about people and cultures. So it's up to you to think for yourself.

Look at these pictures of television "families." Do they seem real to you? Why or why not?

Find Out

If you watch television, you can find your own examples of stereotypes. You could make a chart like this one to record evidence of stereotypes you find in television programs and commercials.

Evidence of Stereotypes on Television

Program/Commercial for:

Character and description:

I think this is a stereotype because:

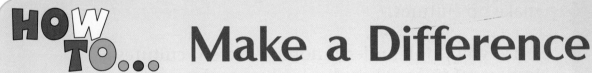

HOW TO... Make a Difference

You can make a difference in your class, your school, and your community. Here's how.

1. **Decide what's important.**
   Choose something that matters to you.

2. **Think of a way to change things.**
   Pick something you can do—a small change can make a big difference.

3. **Make a plan.**
   Figure out what you need for your project and how to do it.

4. **Act on your plan.**
   Get going and make a difference!

Try This

In a group, develop a plan to make sure that stereotypes don't spread in your class this year. Then, act on your plan!

Think For Yourself

At the beginning of this section, we asked this BIG QUESTION:

• *Do you think television helps to spread stereotypes?*

What is your opinion? What facts and examples have you read that support your opinion? What evidence have you collected for yourself? Discuss your opinion with a partner, then share your ideas with the class.

Looking Back

In this chapter, you learned some things about getting along. You also began to discover some of the things that make up cultures.

Do you think understanding different cultures is important in social studies? Why or why not?

Chapter 2

Describing Your World

Where in the world are you?

Right now you might be in your classroom. Your classroom is in one community on the planet earth. Imagine you want to describe where your community is to someone else. How would you do that?

One way to describe where you are is to point to the **location** (where it is) on a map. In this chapter, you can learn how to make and read maps, including maps of the world.

Making a Map

An **inquiry** is one kind of investigation we do in social studies. In an inquiry, we ask questions. Then we find facts and examples that describe what things are like now or were like in the past.

In this chapter, the BIG QUESTION for our inquiry is:

- *How do maps help us describe the world?*

Maps

A **map** is a way of showing information about a place. For example, some maps show the location of towns and roads or mountains and rivers. Other maps show what plants grow in an area or how many people live there. Some maps show more than one type of information.

People use maps for many purposes. For example, you might use a map of a park to find out where to camp for the night. You might use a map of a country to find out how to drive from one city to another.

When you make a map, you have to know what the map will be used for. Then you can decide what information to include. Let's see how to make a map that might help new students at West Lake Elementary School.

A View from the Air

A map usually shows a place from above. This is the view you would see if you were a bird flying over the school or if you took a photograph from an airplane.

A map of a small area such as a school is sometimes called a **plan**.

Try This

Think of something that you would *really* like to know about maps. Write down your question. Make your question a SMALL QUESTION that you can answer with one or two facts.

As you read this chapter, see if you can find the answer to your question. (It may or may not be there!)

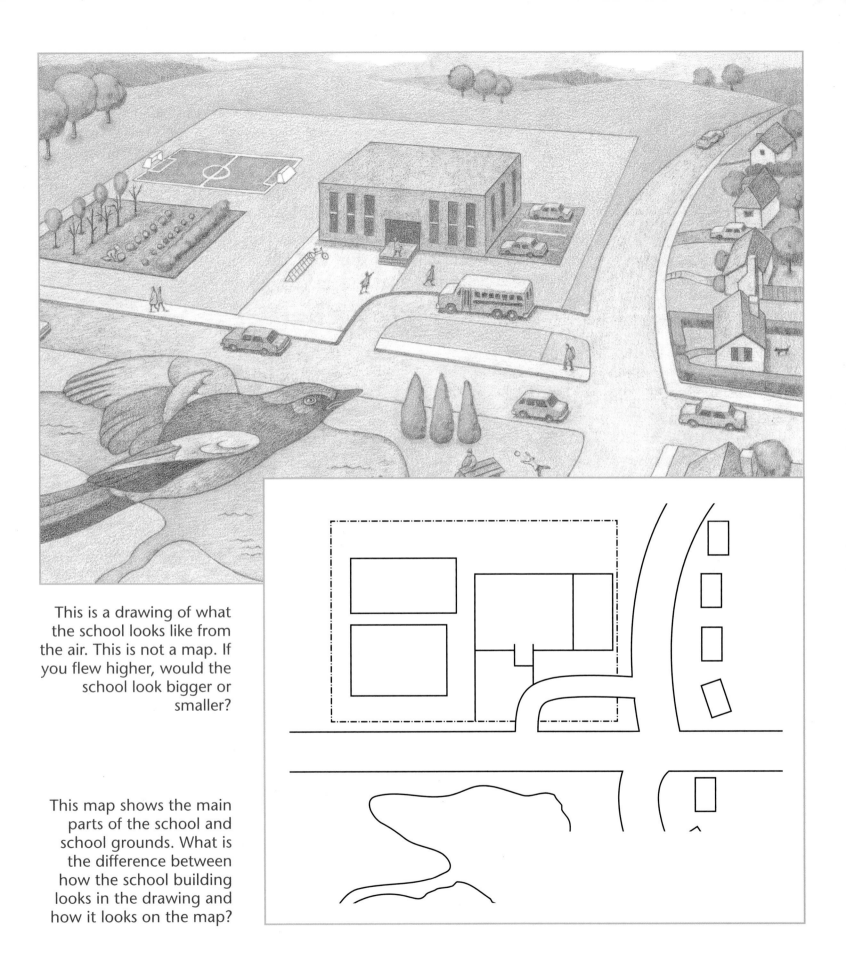

This is a drawing of what the school looks like from the air. This is not a map. If you flew higher, would the school look bigger or smaller?

This map shows the main parts of the school and school grounds. What is the difference between how the school building looks in the drawing and how it looks on the map?

Symbols, Colours, and Labels

If you have seen a map before, you'll notice that our map of the school on page 17 is missing some important parts. If you were a new student, you might have trouble finding out where the school bus stops or where you could park your bike. You might also want to know the names of the streets around the school.

How do we get all of this information on a map? Map-makers use **symbols** to stand for important features. For example, a drawing of an airplane shows the location of the airport. Map-makers also use **labels** to give the names you need to know. They also use colours in the same way in every part of the map. For example, a map-maker might decide that green always stands for grass.

Where does the school bus stop? What is the difference between a symbol and the way something looks in real life?

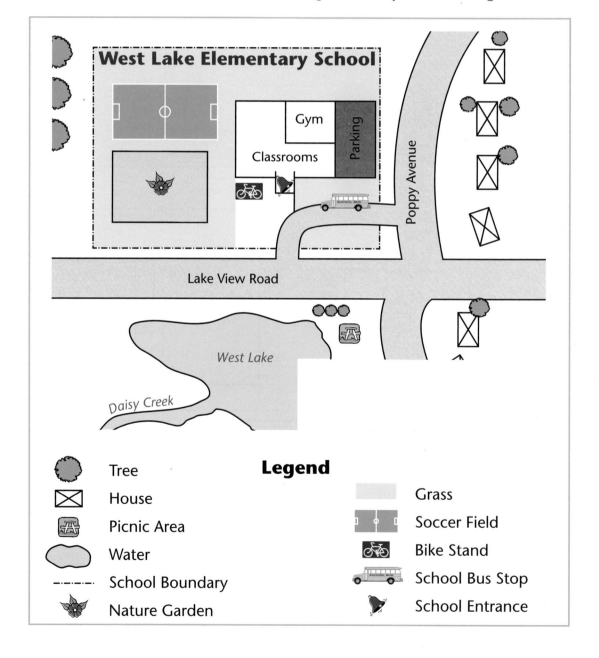

West Lake Elementary School

Gym

Classrooms

Parking

Poppy Avenue

Lake View Road

West Lake

Daisy Creek

Legend

Tree		Grass		
House		Soccer Field		
Picnic Area		Bike Stand		
Water		School Bus Stop		
School Boundary		School Entrance		
Nature Garden				

To read a map, you need to know what symbols and colours the map-maker has chosen. This information is found in a **legend** included with the map. The map of West Lake Elementary School on page 18 has the missing information filled in.

Smaller than Real Life

Most maps are a lot smaller than the places they show. The map-maker has to decide how much smaller than real life the features on the map will be. This is called the **scale** of the map.

For example, the map-maker might decide that 1 centimetre on the map will stand for 10 kilometres in real life. The scale stays the same for all parts of the map.

To make it easy to read the map, the scale usually includes a line that shows you exactly how long 10 kilometres looks on the map.

Grid Codes

A **grid** is a way of using numbers and letters to locate a place on a map. The illustration on this page shows you how it works. The bell is at **grid code** B3.

This is one way to show scale.

0 20 40 60 80 100m

What are the grid codes for the other objects shown here?

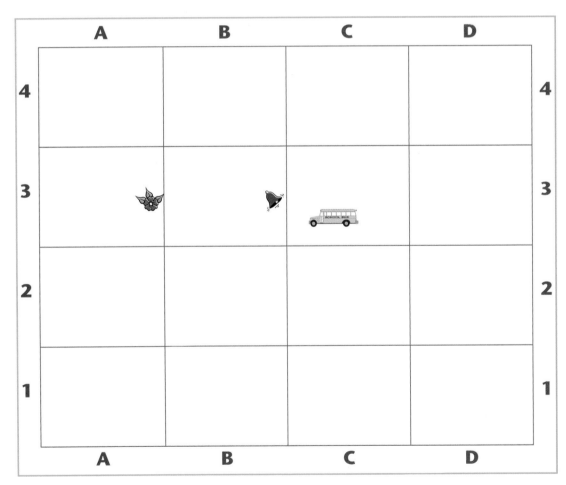

Now the map has a grid and a scale. What is the grid code for the bike stand? How many metres is it from the bus stop to the nature garden? (To figure this out, you can use a ruler. Or you can cut a piece of paper the same length as the scale and use it to measure the distance on the map.)

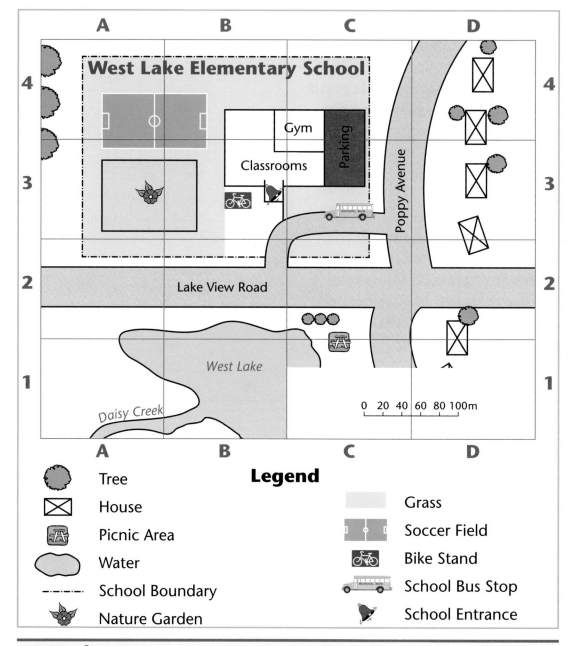

Legend

Tree

House

Picnic Area

Water

----- School Boundary

Nature Garden

Grass

Soccer Field

Bike Stand

School Bus Stop

School Entrance

Think For Yourself

1. Take a good look at the finished map of West Lake Elementary School. Is it a useful map? Write down evidence to support your opinion. If you think the map could be improved, explain how.

    When you explain your ideas and evidence, use mapping words such as *symbol* and *grid*.

2. Share your opinions, evidence, and ideas in a group. After everyone has had a chance to speak, make a list of "Five Signs of a Useful Map" that you can use when you make maps.

Mapping the World

All maps of the world show the basic shapes of the **continents** and **oceans**. Continents are large areas of land. Oceans are large bodies of salt water that separate the continents.

Globes

The world is round, so the best way to show the shapes of the continents and oceans is on a **globe**. A globe is a model of the world that is shaped like a ball.

If you were to look at earth from space, it has no right way up. To make it easier to talk about directions, globes show the North Pole at the top and the South Pole at the bottom.

The problem with a globe is that you can't carry it around with you! What you need is a map.

On a globe, the North and South poles are shown by the rod that goes through the middle and holds the globe in place. The poles give us the directions *north* and *south*. When you look at the globe this way, the direction to your left is *west*. The direction to your right is *east*.

Flat Maps

How can we transfer the surface of a globe onto a flat piece of paper to create a map?

Map-makers do this by breaking the surface of the earth into even pieces. These pieces are then laid beside each other to show the general shape of the continents and oceans. This creates some blank spaces, though, so some pieces have to be stretched or filled in to make the map look complete.

Maps of the World

When we make a flat map of the world, we don't have a rod going through the middle of it to show north and south, the way we do on a globe. Because of this, some maps have a **directional symbol**. This is an arrow that points to the north. East is to the right and west is to the left of north. South is the opposite direction of north.

It is also hard to show the North and South poles clearly, so these are often included in two smaller maps with the main map.

This map shows the world on a flat piece of paper. The Pacific Ocean is in the centre. There is a complete map of the world on pages 24 to 25.

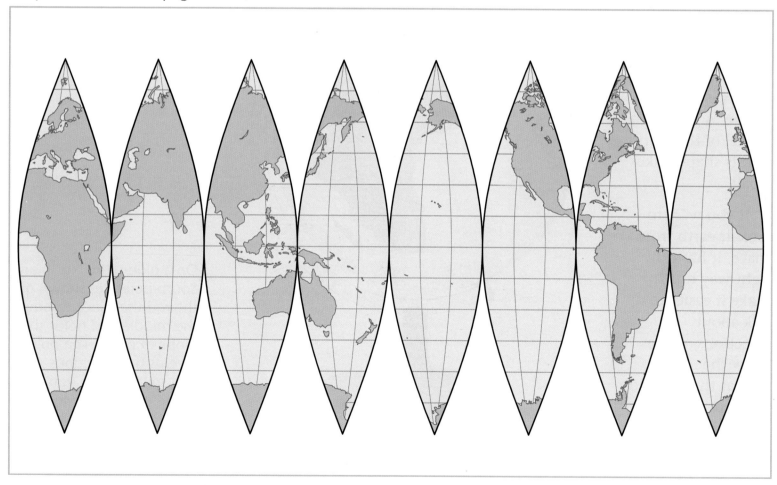

Read a Map

1. Look for a title. This tells you what the map is about.

World Map

2. See if there is a directional symbol on the map. This tells you where to find north.

N

3. Find the scale. This compares the distance on a map to the actual distance in a real place.

0   1000   2000   3000 km

4. Find the legend. This tells you what the symbols and colours on the map mean. Sometimes a legend is called a **key**. To be sure that you understand the legend, try to find one example of each symbol on the map.

Legend

⛰ High Mountains

🌲 Forest

🌳 Savannah

🌴 Tropical Forest

▦ Prairie

▨ Desert

▤ Marsh

▦ Tundra

▨ Ice on Land

▨ Ice on the Sea

🏙 Large Built-up Areas

Try This

Here are some brain teasers about continents and oceans. These questions all ask you for facts. Use the map on pages 24 to 25 to figure out the answers. Then make up some brain teasers of your own to try on your family and friends.

- *Which continent is the biggest?*
- *How many continent names begin with the letter A?*
- *Which continents are all or partly in the Southern Hemisphere?*
- *How many oceans are there in the world?*
- *Which oceans surround North America?*

World Map

The **Equator** is an imaginary line that circles the earth halfway between the North and South poles. It divides the world into the **Northern Hemisphere** and the **Southern Hemisphere**. *Hemisphere* means "half of the world."

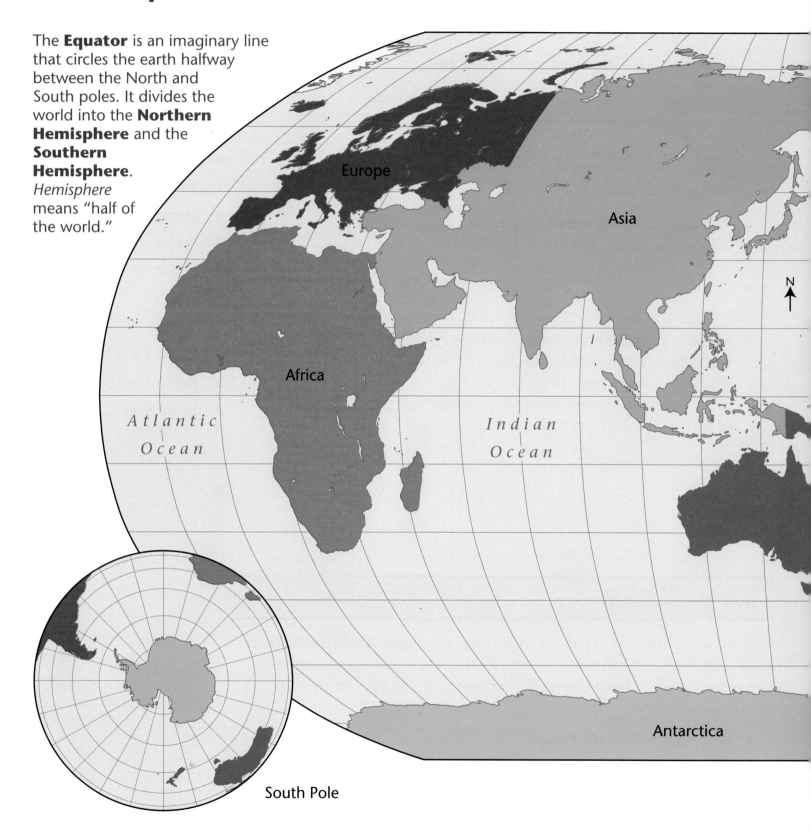

Europe

Asia

N

Africa

Atlantic Ocean

Indian Ocean

Antarctica

South Pole

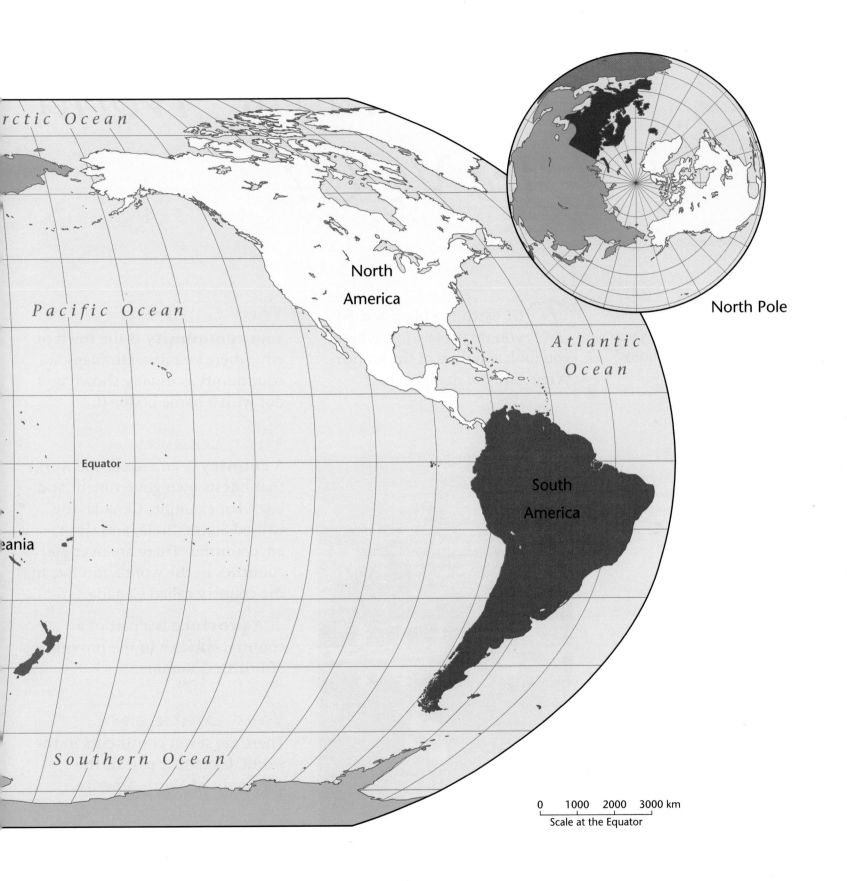

Arctic Ocean

Pacific Ocean

North America

Atlantic Ocean

North Pole

Equator

Oceania

South America

Southern Ocean

0   1000   2000   3000 km
Scale at the Equator

Where in the World Are YOU?

What is the name of your community?

The earth is a big place. So you might feel lost when you look at a map of the world. Where are *you* in all of this?

Your Community

Your **community** is the town or city where you live. On maps, a community is usually shown as a dot with a name beside it.

Your Country

A **country** is an area of the world that has its own government and laws. For example, Canada, the United States, India, and China are countries. There are over 200 countries in the world. You live in the country called Canada.

A **province** is a part of a country. You live in the province of British Columbia.

Your Continent

There are seven continents in the world. Canada is part of the continent of North America.

Victoria is the capital of British Columbia. What does this photo tell you that you can't tell from a map?

These four maps show exactly where the community of Victoria is in the world. What is the difference between the maps? Here's a hint: Look at the scale on each map. Which map shows the most detail? Which map gives you the "big picture"?

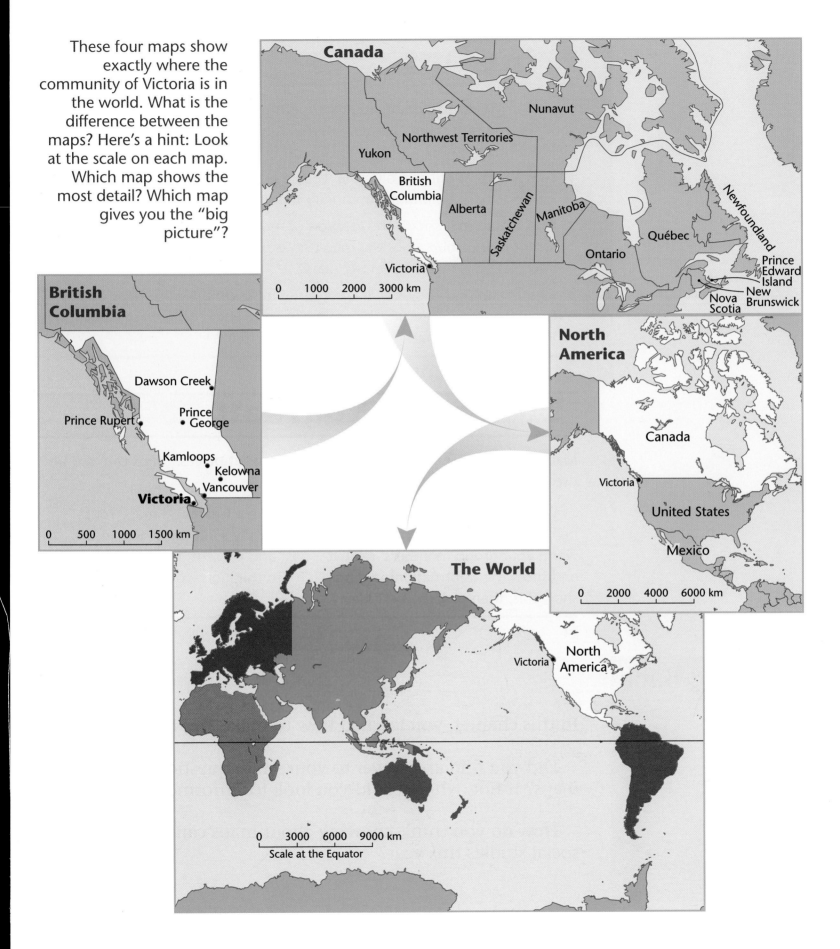

Canada

Nunavut

Northwest Territories

Yukon

British Columbia

Alberta

Saskatchewan

Manitoba

Newfoundland

Québec

Ontario

Prince Edward Island

New Brunswick

Nova Scotia

Victoria

0   1000   2000   3000 km

British Columbia

Dawson Creek

Prince Rupert

Prince George

Kamloops

Kelowna

Vancouver

Victoria

0   500   1000   1500 km

North America

Canada

Victoria

United States

Mexico

0   2000   4000   6000 km

The World

North America

Victoria

0   3000   6000   9000 km
Scale at the Equator

Find Out

Go on a map treasure hunt. You can find maps in **atlases** that might be in your classroom or school library. An atlas is a book that includes many different maps.

1. Find a map of British Columbia. Locate your community on the map. If it isn't on the map, find a community that is nearby.

2. Find a map that shows the location of mountains in Canada. What symbols or colours does the map use to show mountains? What other information is included on the map?

3. Find a map that shows all the countries in North America. How can you tell where the borders of the countries are? Which is the biggest country? What other information is included on the map?

Think For Yourself

Maps aren't only used to show information about places. Maps can also be used to show information about people.

Form a group and figure out a way to make a **heritage** map. Your heritage is all the different cultures of your family. Find out where in the world your group members' relatives, past and present, have come from, and show this information on a map. (Try to think of two different ways to show this, then pick the best idea.)

Looking Back

In this chapter, you learned how to make and read maps.

Did you find an answer to your small question about maps? If not, where could you look for information?

How do you think knowing about maps can help you in social studies this year?

Chapter 3

Living in the World

Imagine it's a crisp autumn day. Could you survive if your school bus broke down four blocks from your house? What if it broke down 20 kilometres away from town in the middle of a forest?

If you're like most people, you'd probably be a little worried if your bus broke down far away from the nearest town. There's a good reason to worry! If you don't have the right clothing, food to eat, and some form of shelter you could be in trouble. These are all **basic needs**. We need them to survive in any situation, even a day at school!

In this chapter, you can learn about some of the ways people meet their basic needs today and in the past.

Survival!

What do think people really need to survive? One way to find out is to imagine what decisions you would make if you were in a tricky situation.

Think For Yourself

Work on this **problem** in a group of three. When you solve a problem, you have to study the situation and decide on the best thing to do.

Your class is returning from a field trip to study the wilderness environment near where you live. It's 2:30 in the afternoon on a cool autumn day. You're driving along an old logging road. Twenty kilometres from town, the school bus breaks down. One of your teachers has a cell phone, but the batteries are dead. You can't call for help, and nobody knows where you are. The only thing to do is to walk to the main highway to get help.

You and your friend volunteer to go with one of the teachers. No one is sure how far you'll have to walk, though. You need to be prepared to spend several hours on the road. You might even have to camp for the night. What will you need for the trip? Here's what's on the bus.

Can opener

Hunting knife

Rope

Tent

Heavy jackets

Juice boxes

Hats

Compass

Flashlight

Chocolate bars

Bottled water

Plastic sheet

Matches

Sleeping bags

Newspaper

NEWS

Local map

Tins of beans

BEANS

Backpack

Dried fruit and nuts

Walkman and CDs

Thick socks

Boots

You can only choose six items for your survival kit. What items would you pick? Give reasons for your choices.

HOW TO... Think About Choices

When you make decisions, try to imagine what will happen if you make one choice or another. Think of **pros** (good things) and **cons** (bad things) for each choice. You might find it helps to list things in a chart like the one shown here.

Pros	Cons

Once you have written down your pros and cons, look them over. Decide which points are really important to you. Think of these points first when you make your decision. Things might be important because of what you know, what you believe, or how you feel.

Weird and Wonderful Places

Reading Hint

If you come to a word you don't know, try to figure it out. Sound out the first three letters, then start the sentence over. When you come to the word again, think about the beginning sound and what word might make sense.

Where do you think would be the toughest place on earth to live? Chances are, somebody calls this place home! Wherever people live, they learn ways to meet their basic needs.

As people live and work together in a community, they develop a culture. Culture includes more than food, shelter, and clothing. Beliefs, art, music, and language are all part of culture. These things help to make each culture special.

When you want to understand a culture, though, looking at the **environment** and basic needs is a good place to start. In this section, you can take a tour of some of the interesting places in the world to live.

Environments

The environment is the natural world of the land, sea, and air. It includes living parts such as plants and animals. It also includes other parts such as soil and water. There are also different ocean environments around the world. Cities are environments that are created by people.

The map on pages 34 to 35 shows different environments around the world. The photos show different cultures.

Try This

In a group, discuss all the ways the environment where you live affects the type of food, shelter, and clothing in your community. You might want to record your ideas in pictures, on a web, or in a list.

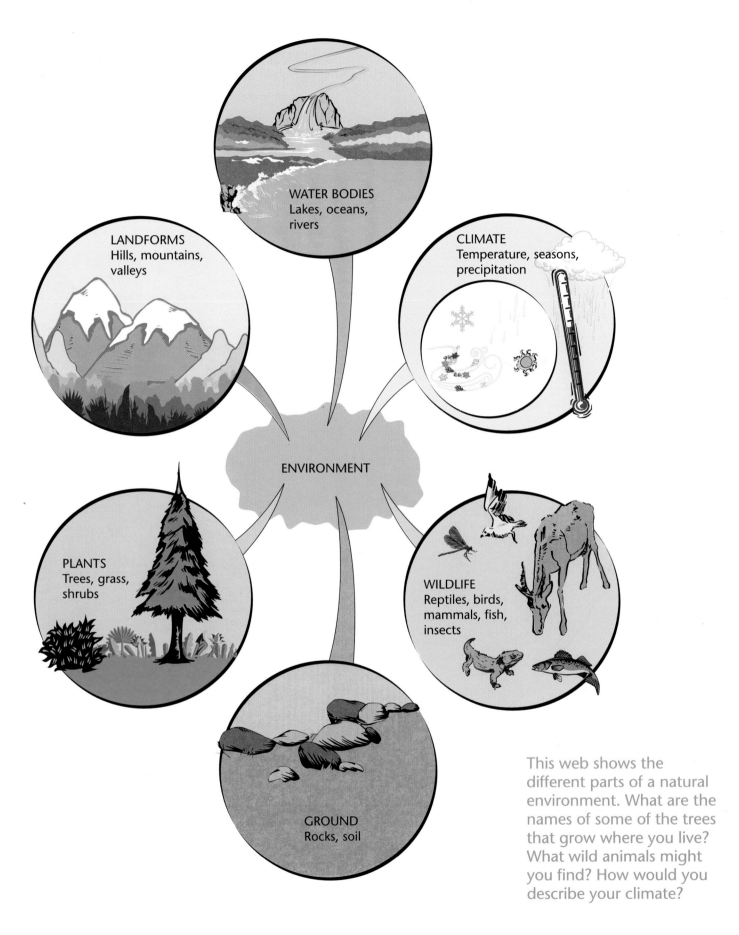

WATER BODIES
Lakes, oceans, rivers

LANDFORMS
Hills, mountains, valleys

CLIMATE
Temperature, seasons, precipitation

ENVIRONMENT

PLANTS
Trees, grass, shrubs

WILDLIFE
Reptiles, birds, mammals, fish, insects

GROUND
Rocks, soil

This web shows the different parts of a natural environment. What are the names of some of the trees that grow where you live? What wild animals might you find? How would you describe your climate?

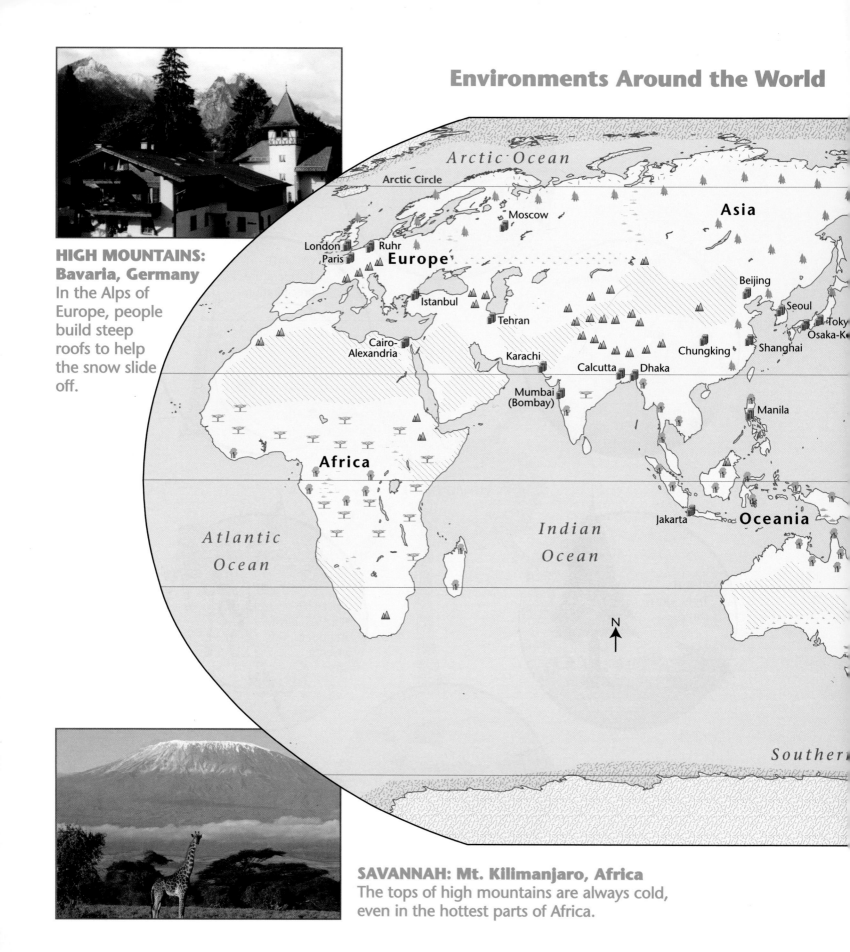

HIGH MOUNTAINS:
Bavaria, Germany
In the Alps of Europe, people build steep roofs to help the snow slide off.

SAVANNAH: Mt. Kilimanjaro, Africa
The tops of high mountains are always cold, even in the hottest parts of Africa.

Arctic Ocean

Arctic Circle

Moscow

Asia

London
Paris
Ruhr
Europe

Istanbul

Beijing

Tehran

Seoul

Cairo-
Alexandria

Osaka-K

Toky

Karachi

Chungking

Shanghai

Calcutta
Dhaka

Mumbai
(Bombay)

Manila

Africa

Jakarta

Oceania

Atlantic Ocean

Indian Ocean

N

Southern

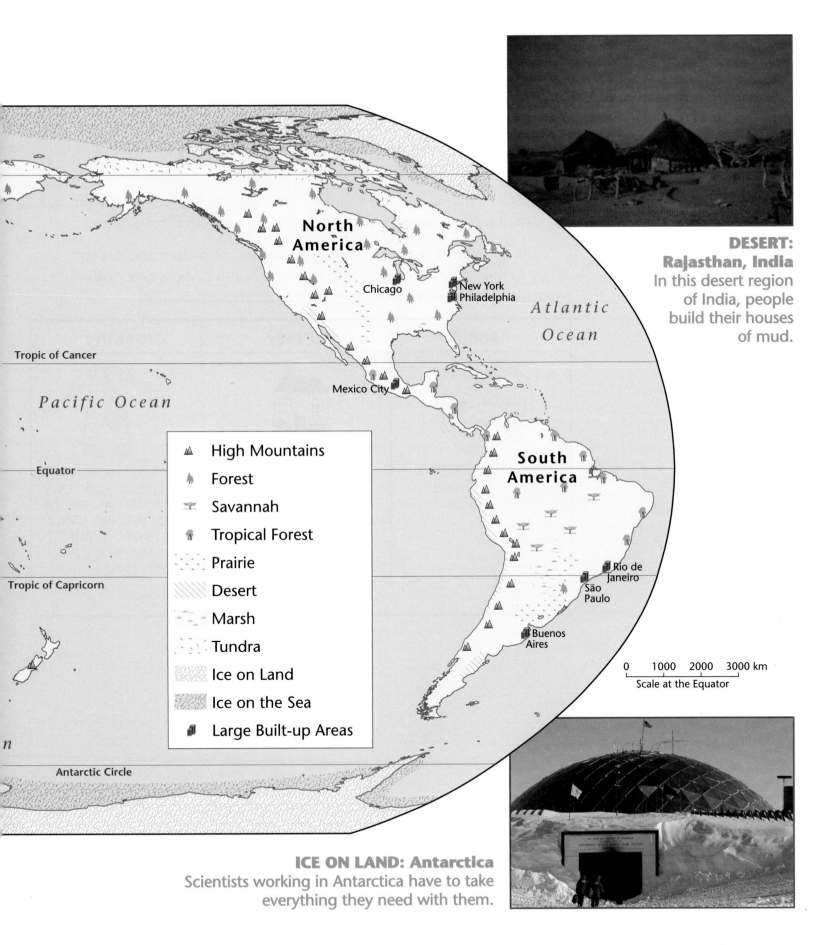

**DESERT:
Rajasthan, India**
In this desert region
of India, people
build their houses
of mud.

*Atlantic
Ocean*

North
America

Chicago

New York
Philadelphia

Tropic of Cancer

Mexico City

Pacific Ocean

Equator

South
America

Tropic of Capricorn

Rio de
Janeiro

São
Paulo

Buenos
Aires

Antarctic Circle

	High Mountains
	Forest
	Savannah
	Tropical Forest
	Prairie
	Desert
	Marsh
	Tundra
	Ice on Land
	Ice on the Sea
	Large Built-up Areas

0   1000   2000   3000 km
Scale at the Equator

ICE ON LAND: Antarctica
Scientists working in Antarctica have to take
everything they need with them.

Find Out

Make a chart to show examples of food, shelter, and clothing from different cultures around the world. You can find information in sources such as books, magazines, and the Internet and by interviewing people. Try to find at least three different examples of each basic need.

Your chart might look like this. Make the squares big enough for pictures. You can draw your own pictures or cut out pictures from magazines.

Write a **caption** that describes each drawing or picture and explain where in the world you would find this type of food, shelter, or clothing. (A caption is the writing that goes with a picture or drawing.)

Food	Shelter	Clothing
Pizza is a dish that first came from Italy.	This is one type of house you would find in Canada.	Many women in Pakistan wear this type of top, called the Shalwar kamiz [Shahl-WAHR kha-MEEZ] over loose pants.

Salmon and the River People

Environments don't only present challenges to people. They also give us everything we need to survive, plus a lot of fun things that we don't need, but like to have!

We call the parts of the environment that are useful to people **natural resources**. Trees, water, fish, and soil are a few examples of natural resources. When we harvest these resources, we make small or big changes to the environment.

In the rest of this chapter, you can learn about the natural resources in the lower Fraser Valley in British Columbia. You'll see how this area went from salmon, to settlers, to city lights!

On maps, the area we are interested in in this section is called the lower Fraser Valley. The Fraser is a large, long river with many small rivers flowing into it.

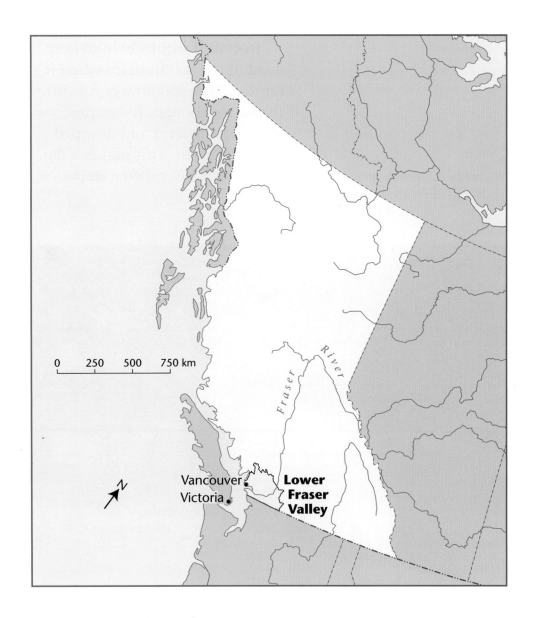

0   250   500   750 km

Fraser River

Vancouver
Victoria
Lower Fraser Valley

Coniferous trees have small needles instead of leaves and stay green all year round.

This is traditional dip-net fishing. How do you think fish are caught?

The Natural Environment

The lower Fraser Valley is part of the BC coastal region. In this region, heavy rains, warm summers, and cool winters are perfect for **coniferous** trees such as cedar, Douglas fir, and hemlock.

The thick forest provides shelter for animals such as deer, bears, and squirrels. Bugs that fall from branches into the rivers are food for fish such as salmon.

Trees and shrubs help to keep most of the soil in place when it rains. A little soil always gets into the water, though. It's carried along by the river and dropped near the ocean. This makes a flat area of rich soil called a **delta**.

The First People

The lower Fraser Valley is the home of the Stó:lō [STO-loe] people. The Stó:lō are one of the **Aboriginal** peoples of Canada. The **ancestors** (relatives in the past) of Aboriginal peoples were the first people to live in North America.

In the past, the Stó:lō fished, hunted animals, and gathered forest plants for food. The forests also provided what they needed for shelter, clothing, and transportation. For example, they wove cedar bark to make skirts and mats.

The Most Important Resource

The salmon in the Fraser River were the resource the Stó:lō valued the most. Good fishing spots were important. Each family had the right to fish in a particular spot and the responsibility to take good care of the fish in that spot.

Technologies

Technologies are the tools we use to meet our basic needs. Technology also includes knowing how to do things.

All the tools used by the Stó:lō in the past were made from the resources in their environment. For example, some of the nets they used for fishing were made from stinging nettle plants that grew in the area.

The Stó:lō had many tools for fishing. These included wooden spears, large nets that they stretched between two boats across the river, and **dip nets**. Although they caught a lot of fish, they never caught all of them. This made sure that some fish could always return to the river to lay their eggs.

Fish was eaten fresh, dried, or smoked. Fish was dried on wooden racks outdoors and smoked on racks over small fires. Smoked and dried fish were kept for times when there weren't a lot of fish in the river.

Ideas About the Environment

In the past, the Stó:lō depended on the environment to meet their basic needs. But they were careful not to change any part of the environment in a big way. This made sure that nature's systems kept working.

The Stó:lō believed that it was important to share resources with each other. They made sure nothing was wasted. Many of the Stó:lō's traditions and beliefs are about respecting nature in this way.

There is a traditional ceremony to honour the first salmon caught each year. The salmon is shared with others, then the bones are returned to the river. This shows respect for the salmon.

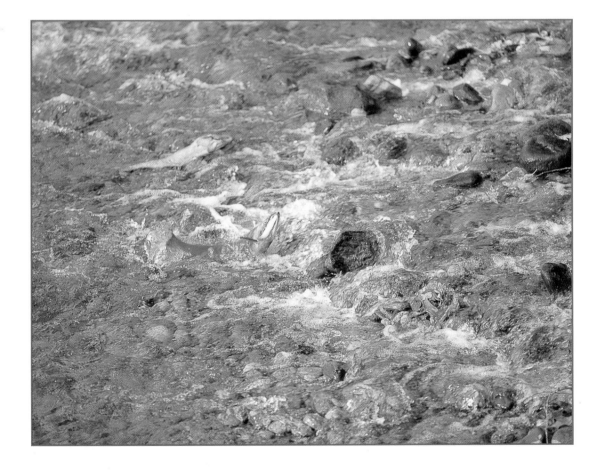

At certain times of the year, salmon return from the ocean to the Fraser River to lay eggs. In the past, millions and millions of salmon returned during these **runs**.

Try This

You've read a lot about the Stó:lō in this section. Try answering a
BIG QUESTION and SMALL QUESTIONS to organize your thoughts.

BIG QUESTION:

- *How did the Stó:lō use the resources in the Fraser Valley?*

SMALL QUESTIONS:

- *In the past, what resource was most important to the Stó:lō?*
- *What are some examples of the technologies they used to get this resource?*
- *What are some of the ways they used the resource?*
- *What were the Stó:lō's ideas about the environment?*
- *Did their actions make big or small changes to the environment?*

HOW TO... Find Main Ideas

Information is usually organized using MAIN IDEAS and *details*. The main
ideas are the important parts of the information. The details give facts
or examples to help you understand the main ideas. Here's an example:

MAIN IDEA:

- The lower Fraser Valley offers many natural resources.

Details:

- The bark of cedar trees can be used to weave mats.
- The rivers in the valley are full of fish.

When you read information, stop from time to time to check that
you know what the main ideas are. Paragraphs often begin by telling
you a main idea. Titles are also good clues. In diagrams, lines often
connect main ideas and details.

From Settlers...

The Stó:lō found a way of living in their environment that met their basic needs. Their actions made only small changes to the environment.

European **settlers** had different ideas about how the lower Fraser Valley could help them meet their basic needs.

Settlers

Around 1860, many people from Europe came to the lower Fraser Valley.

There had been European traders and miners in the area for many years, but they weren't interested in setting up homes. The European settlers were different. They wanted to stay in the area and farm.

The Most Important Resource

The settlers hunted and fished for some of their food, but to them the important resource was the flat land with its rich soil. This was perfect for farming. They wanted to plant crops and raise animals.

Traders wanted furs. The miners were looking for gold. These are two other resources in the lower Fraser Valley.

This shows a settlement in the Fraser Valley around 1880. What European technologies do you see?

Technologies

The settlers brought metal tools with them. Axes, shovels, and picks were needed to chop down the trees and clear the land. Once the land was cleared, they used horses or oxen to pull ploughs.

Many of the other things the settlers used, such as cloth for clothing and pots for cooking, also came from Europe.

The settlers knew all about farming and how to use the products of the farm. For example, they dried grass to make hay. This gave their animals food for the winter. The settlers knew that some crops, such as potatoes, would keep all winter if they were stored in a cool, dry place. They also dried and smoked meat and made milk into food such as cheese.

Ideas About the Environment

The settlers came from a culture that believed farming was the best way to make sure everyone got enough to eat. They saw the natural environment of the area as something wild and not very useful.

The settlers wanted to change the natural environment so they could farm. They worked their farms carefully so that the soil stayed rich. They used the land well so that there was no waste.

Try This

Remember the set of questions you answered to make sure you understood the main ideas about the Stó:lō? Now answer the same kind of questions about the settlers.

BIG QUESTION:
- *How did the settlers use the resources in the Fraser Valley?*

SMALL QUESTIONS:
- *What resources were most important to the settlers?*
- *What are some examples of the technologies they used on their farms?*
- *What are some of the ways they used the crops and animals they raised?*
- *What were their ideas about the environment?*
- *Did their actions make big or small changes to the environment?*

To City Lights

Today, the lower Fraser Valley is the centre of two big **issues**. One is to do with farmland. The other is to do with fishing.

An issue is a situation that doesn't have one right solution. Instead, people have different **points of view** about the best thing to do. A point of view is a way of thinking about something.

Sometimes you might be asked to give your opinion about the best solution to an issue. Before you make your decision, you should collect information about the different points of view. This will help you make sure you form a fair opinion. In this section, you can collect information about the Fraser Valley today.

Modern Farms

In time, the settlers took over most of the land from the Stó:lō. Farms grew bigger and bigger.

The Stó:lō had to move onto small areas of land called **reserves**.

This is a dairy farm in the lower Fraser Valley. Most land in British Columbia isn't good for farming. Some people think that farming is the best use of this part of the province.

New technologies, such as tractors and ploughs, made farming more and more efficient. Today, little of the natural environment is left. Now it is mostly farms.

City Lights

Now, some people want to change the Fraser Valley again. They want to build houses on the farmland. Cities in the area, such as Vancouver and New Westminster, don't have enough homes for all the people who want to live there. The flat land that is so good for farming is also the easiest land to build houses on.

Other people value the farmland in the lower Fraser Valley. They say that the land is needed to grow food for all of the people in the cities. They want it to be illegal to build houses on Fraser Valley farmland. This is an issue that needs to be worked out.

What About the Stó:lō?

Many Stó:lō still live in the lower Fraser Valley. They work at a variety of jobs, including fishing.

Today, the Canadian government makes the laws about fishing in the Fraser River. But many Stó:lō believe that they should have some say in these matters, too. They explain that they had traditional rights to these areas for thousands of years before the Europeans came. Many fishers who are not Stó:lō think everyone should follow the government's laws. This is another issue that needs to be worked out.

This photograph of the lower Fraser Valley was taken from the air. How can you tell what parts are farmland?

Today, there are far fewer salmon in the Fraser River than there were in the past. This is because changes to the environment have polluted the water and blocked off streams. Modern fishing methods have also made it easy to catch a lot of fish at once.

Think For Yourself

This chart shows you two points of view about selling farmland to build houses. Consider both points of view. Think of the pros and cons of each, then give your opinion. You might want to do this in an **oral presentation**.

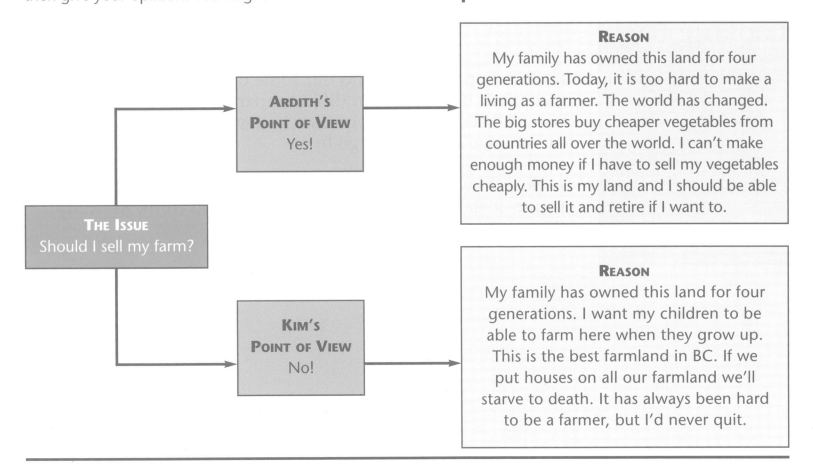

THE ISSUE
Should I sell my farm?

ARDITH'S POINT OF VIEW
Yes!

REASON
My family has owned this land for four generations. Today, it is too hard to make a living as a farmer. The world has changed. The big stores buy cheaper vegetables from countries all over the world. I can't make enough money if I have to sell my vegetables cheaply. This is my land and I should be able to sell it and retire if I want to.

KIM'S POINT OF VIEW
No!

REASON
My family has owned this land for four generations. I want my children to be able to farm here when they grow up. This is the best farmland in BC. If we put houses on all our farmland we'll starve to death. It has always been hard to be a farmer, but I'd never quit.

 **Make an Oral Presentation**

When you make an oral presentation, make sure you organize your ideas before you start. Here's one way to do it.

1. Start by explaining your MAIN IDEA. Make this short, but clear.

2. Give some facts and examples to help people understand your main idea.

3. Finish by reminding people about your main idea.

   When you speak, don't rush. Speak clearly and look at your audience. (Some people find it helps to take a few deep breaths before they begin an oral presentation!)

Looking Back

In this chapter, you found out some of the ways people meet their basic needs in different parts of the world. When you read about the lower Fraser Valley, you saw how things can change as the years go by.

How do you think understanding environments will help you in social studies this year? Why do you think we study the past as well as the present?

Chapter 4

SINCE THE BEGINNING OF TIME

The Elders tell us that Aboriginal peoples have lived in North America "since the beginning of time"—for so long that people think of it as forever.

Can you imagine what it was like to live in your community before there were any modern technologies? Imagine: no roads, no supermarkets, and no video games! Instead, imagine hiking through thick forests or green grasslands, canoeing down fast rivers, and fishing on clear blue lakes.

In this chapter, you can begin to find out what life was like for Aboriginal peoples in the past. Learning about the past can help you understand traditions and values that are important to Aboriginal peoples today.

LIVING OFF THE LAND

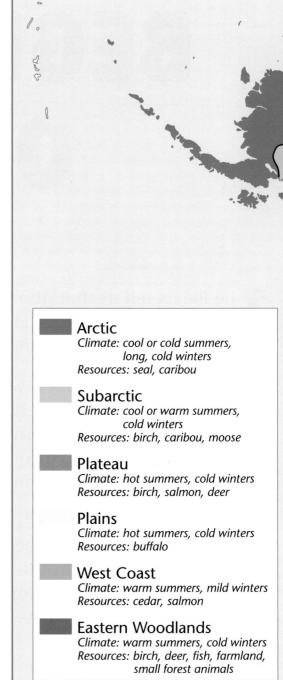

Canada includes many different environments. Wherever they lived, Aboriginal peoples in the past used the natural resources in their environment to meet their basic needs.

This map shows the resources that were *most important* to people in each region. It doesn't show all the resources they used. What resources were important where you live? Are these resources important today?

Arctic
Climate: cool or cold summers, long, cold winters
Resources: seal, caribou

Subarctic
Climate: cool or warm summers, cold winters
Resources: birch, caribou, moose

Plateau
Climate: hot summers, cold winters
Resources: birch, salmon, deer

Plains
Climate: hot summers, cold winters
Resources: buffalo

West Coast
Climate: warm summers, mild winters
Resources: cedar, salmon

Eastern Woodlands
Climate: warm summers, cold winters
Resources: birch, deer, fish, farmland, small forest animals

Try This

Here is a list of some of the technologies used by Aboriginal peoples in the past. Use the information on the map to figure out which technology you would find in which region. You might find one technology in more than one region.

- large houses made of cedar
- scarecrows to keep birds away from crops
- birch bark canoes
- teepees made of buffalo hide
- sealskin mittens

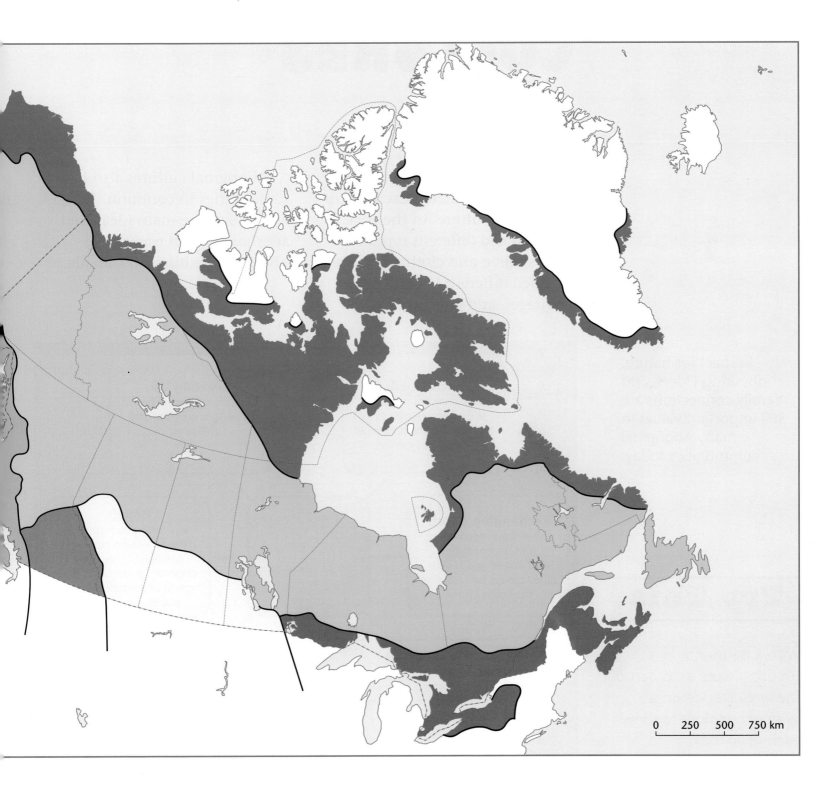

LEARNING ABOUT CULTURES

There are many Aboriginal groups in Canada. Each group has its own culture. In the past, this included different types of food, shelter, and clothing. It also included different beliefs, languages, and governments.

Aboriginal cultures also had some things in common. This web shows the main ideas that are shared by all traditional Aboriginal cultures in Canada.

Respect for nature, honouring Elders, and family connections are still important values in many Aboriginal communities today.

Try This

With a partner or in a group, discuss each part of the web. Decide on a symbol or colour to show each main idea.

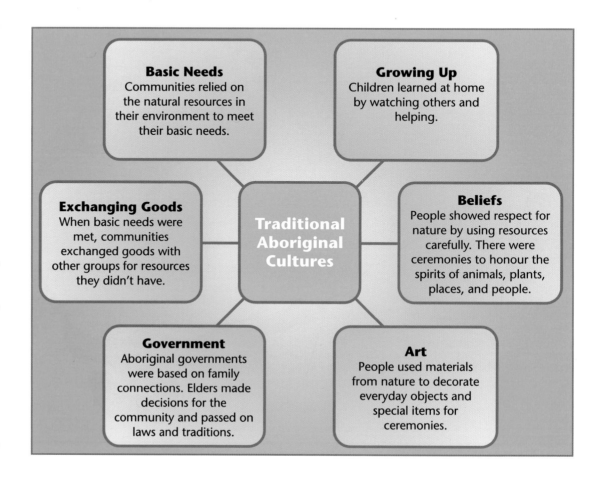

Basic Needs
Communities relied on the natural resources in their environment to meet their basic needs.

Growing Up
Children learned at home by watching others and helping.

Exchanging Goods
When basic needs were met, communities exchanged goods with other groups for resources they didn't have.

Traditional Aboriginal Cultures

Beliefs
People showed respect for nature by using resources carefully. There were ceremonies to honour the spirits of animals, plants, places, and people.

Government
Aboriginal governments were based on family connections. Elders made decisions for the community and passed on laws and traditions.

Art
People used materials from nature to decorate everyday objects and special items for ceremonies.

THE COPPER INUIT

In the rest of this chapter, you can learn about the traditional culture of the Copper Inuit. You'll find out how to make a sled out of fish, how to cook your food with no wood or electricity, and why Inuit kids don't have to eat their vegetables!

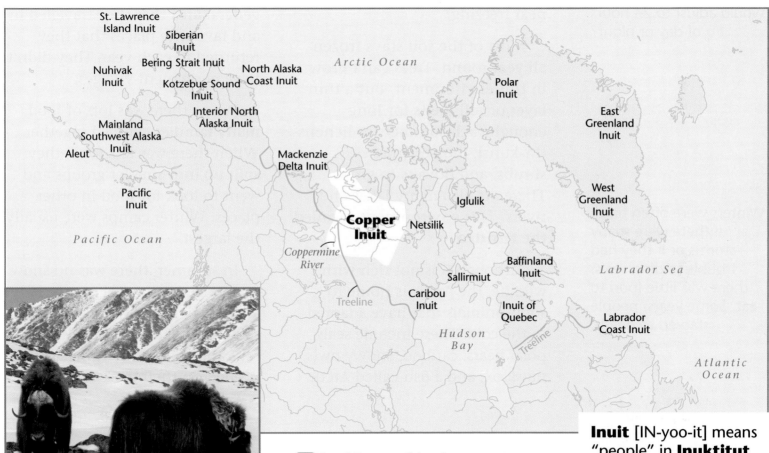

St. Lawrence Island Inuit

Siberian Inuit

Bering Strait Inuit

Nuhivak Inuit

North Alaska Coast Inuit

Kotzebue Sound Inuit

Arctic Ocean

Polar Inuit

Interior North Alaska Inuit

Mainland Southwest Alaska Inuit

East Greenland Inuit

Aleut

Mackenzie Delta Inuit

Pacific Inuit

Iglulik

West Greenland Inuit

Copper Inuit

Netsilik

Pacific Ocean

Coppermine River

Labrador Sea

Baffinland Inuit

Sallirmiut

Treeline

Caribou Inuit

Inuit of Quebec

Labrador Coast Inuit

Hudson Bay

Treeline

Atlantic Ocean

Musk ox look fierce, but they are quite mild-mannered. Their Inuktitut name is *umingmak* [u-MING-mak], meaning "bearded one."

The "Copper" in the name **Copper Inuit** comes from the fact that small amounts of copper metal lie near the surface of the earth along the Coppermine River. The people who lived in the area dug the copper from the ground

Inuit [IN-yoo-it] means "people" in **Inuktitut** [in-UK-ti-tut], the language spoken by the Inuit. One person is called an **Inuk** [in-OOK]. In the past, these people were called Eskimos.

In the middle of winter, the sun never comes up. It isn't completely dark, though. The stars and moon light the sky. In the middle of summer, the sun never sets, so there's light all day and all night. How do you think you would adjust to 24 hours of day or night?

Winters were often hard. If there were many storms or if they had trouble finding seals, there was little food to eat. Some years, people starved to death.

Summer was a fun time. In mid-summer, it was light all the time, so people stayed up or slept whenever they wanted! Children played a lot of games.

and pounded it into tools such as needles and knives. Few Aboriginal groups could get metal so easily.

The Environment

The Arctic is very cold and dry. Winters last for a long time—about nine months of the year. In the central Arctic, ice forms over the ocean in winter. Even in the middle of summer it is cool, with the temperature often remaining near freezing.

Most of the soil stays frozen all year round. Trees can't grow in this environment. But a thin layer of soil melts for long enough each summer for lichens [LY-kuns], mosses, grasses, shrubs, and flowers to grow. There are also many lakes and rivers. This environment is called the **tundra**.

Although it is not rich with wildlife, the Arctic is home to some animals that have adapted to the cold. These include seals, polar bears, caribou, snowy owls, musk ox, and a fish called Arctic

char. **Waterfowl** (ducks, geese, and swans) and other birds fly up from the south for the summer.

Their Communities

In the past, the Copper Inuit lived in small groups that kept moving during the year in search of food and other resources. They moved every month or so in winter and every few days in summer.

Groups of families had a general area that they travelled in and favourite places that they returned to each year. They didn't have permanent villages.

When there was lots of food, many families camped together. When there was less food, they split up into smaller groups and went to look for food in other places. Winter camps were usually the largest.

In summer, there was no snow for the sleds to travel on, so sleds and heavy goods were left in a safe place. Families travelled on foot and carried the things they needed on their backs.

Find Out

Some families used a type of boat called a **kayak** [KY-ak] to travel in summer. Find out what a traditional Copper Inuit kayak looked like and how it was made. You might want to make a model kayak to show the results of your research.

The Seasonal Food Cycle

The two most important resources the Copper Inuit used to meet their basic needs were **ringed seals** and **barren ground caribou**. They organized their year around hunting these two animals.

Winter

In winter, they lived on the ice over the ocean and hunted the seals that lived beneath the ice.

Spring

Before the ice melted in spring, families moved onto the land. Most people went to good spots to fish for trout and Arctic char.

The catch was dried and stored in **caches** [kash-UZ] (safe places under rocks). It was picked up later in autumn when the snow came and people were once again able to travel by sled.

Summer

Families chose their summer routes depending on the resources they wanted. Some people went to places where they could collect copper or **soapstone** (a soft rock that was easy to carve). Others travelled south to the **treeline** to get wood.

As they travelled, the Copper Inuit trapped birds and small animals. Sometimes they caught musk ox. They also collected duck and geese eggs as well as roots and berries. In August, they began following and hunting caribou herds.

In winter and spring, the Copper Inuit used sleds when they travelled. This picture shows a sled with runners made of wood. Wood was valuable, so runners might also be made from bones, antlers, or even a row of frozen fish rolled up in caribou hide! Why do you think wood was so valuable in the Arctic?

The treeline is the northern point in the environment at which trees can no longer grow.

The Copper Inuit traded copper, soapstone, wood, and caribou hides. In turn, they hoped to get resources they didn't have in their area, such as **iron pyrites** (a type of rock that is good for starting fires) and polar bear skins.

The Inuit call ringed seals nattik [NAHT-teek]. Caribou are called tuktu [tuk-TU].

To catch a ringed seal, a hunter looked for air holes. Then he sat and waited for the seal to come up for air. Sometimes a hunter waited for eight or ten hours in weather as cold as -40°C! What does the picture show you about how seals were killed?

Autumn

In late autumn, people gathered at the shore. They ate fish and meat that had been dried during the summer. They prepared for winter by making tools and clothing. Sometimes they traded with other groups.

Once the ocean was frozen, the Copper Inuit moved out onto the ice to begin the cycle again.

Ringed Seals

Ringed seals were an important resource for the Copper Inuit. The seals spend the winter under the

sea ice. They come up to breathe through the air holes in the ice.

Although they also ate the meat, seal **blubber** (fat) was prized by the Inuit for food. Oil made from blubber was also burned for heat and light. Sealskins were both tough and waterproof. They were used to make things such as buckets and boots.

Barren Ground Caribou

Barren ground caribou live in large herds. (Barren ground is another name for tundra.) Some herds live all year in the Arctic. Others spend the winter in the forests further south and **migrate** to the tundra for the summer.

Caribou were very useful to the Inuit. Hides were used to make clothing, dog harnesses, and bags. Caribou meat was a good food source. Bones and antlers were used to make tent frames, sled runners, and small tools. The **sinews** [SIH-nyooz] along the animal's back were used to make thread. (Sinews are long strands of tissue that connect muscles to bones.)

When raw, seal blubber and seal meat are rich in vitamins other people get from vegetables. The Inuit only cooked their meat a little, and often ate it raw. Seal and caribou are still popular foods in the Arctic.

When they migrate, birds and animals move from one place to another.

By August, caribou have a fine, warm coat. As the weather gets colder, their coats get heavier and stiffer. The Copper Inuit made work clothes from heavier hides. Fancy clothes were made from lighter ones.

The hardest part about hunting caribou is catching up with them! One way the Copper Inuit did this was to have women and children howl like wolves and chase the caribou to the waiting hunters. What type of weapon is the hunter using in this picture?

Make a diagram that shows the resources gathered or hunted by the Copper Inuit in the Coppermine River area during each season. You could use words, pictures, or both. A **flow chart** like the one shown here is one way to organize your information.

You'll need to **skim** this section to find the information for your chart.

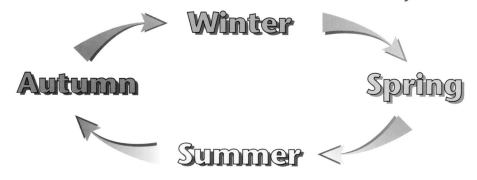

HOW TO... Skim to Find Information

Skimming is a special way of reading. It can help you save time when you want to locate ideas, facts, and examples. Here's how to skim.

1. Write down the **key words** that might help you find the information you need. A key word might be a name, a word from the question you are asking, or a word that is connected to the main idea.

2. When you start looking for information, go slowly, but don't read every word. Move your eyes down the page looking for your key words. Pay special attention to headings. They tell you what the next paragraphs are about.

3. When you come to a key word, read more carefully. Look for ideas, facts, and examples that you want to write down or sketch.

KEEPING WARM

In the Arctic, if you can't keep warm you can't survive! The Inuit developed efficient types of shelter and clothing to protect them from the weather. In this section, you can find out what was special about the Copper Inuit's clothing and shelter. You can also look at some modern Inuit art.

Clothing

You might have noticed by looking at the pictures in this chapter that people wore clothing made from animal hides. In the Copper Inuit culture, most tops and pants were made of caribou skins. Sometimes in summer, though, people wore light clothing made of sealskins. Summer clothing helped protect people's skin from biting flies.

In winter, the Copper Inuit wore two layers of clothing. The first layer was worn with the fur against the skin. This inner layer

The Copper Inuit believed it was bad luck to sew new caribou hides when living over the ocean. So all caribou-skin clothing had to be made by the end of autumn before the people moved onto the ice.

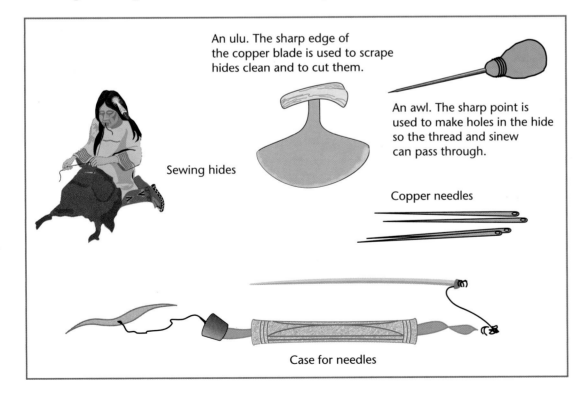

An ulu. The sharp edge of the copper blade is used to scrape hides clean and to cut them.

An awl. The sharp point is used to make holes in the hide so the thread and sinew can pass through.

Sewing hides

Copper needles

Case for needles

Hides and sealskins were cleaned and dried, then cut into clothing shapes. Clothing was sewn with wet sinew. As the sinews dried, the seams closed tighter.

Snow goggles were like sunglasses. If people didn't wear them in the spring, the bright light on the snow could cause them to go blind.

was usually made from the softer caribou hides obtained in early autumn. The second layer was worn with the fur on the outside. The outer layer was made from the heavier late-autumn hides. Warm air got trapped between the two layers of clothing. This helped to keep the people warm.

Boots were usually made of sealskin. Sealskin is not warm, but it is waterproof. For warmth, people lined their boots with fur.

Shelter

In spring, the Copper Inuit lived in heavy tents made of caribou hide. When they stored their sleds for the summer, they switched to small tents made of lighter hides.

In winter, the Copper Inuit built houses out of blocks of snow. This type of house is usually called an **igloo**. (*Igloo* is the Inuktitut word for any type of house.) An igloo big enough for a small family could be built by two people in about an hour. A large igloo was built by connecting many rooms with passages.

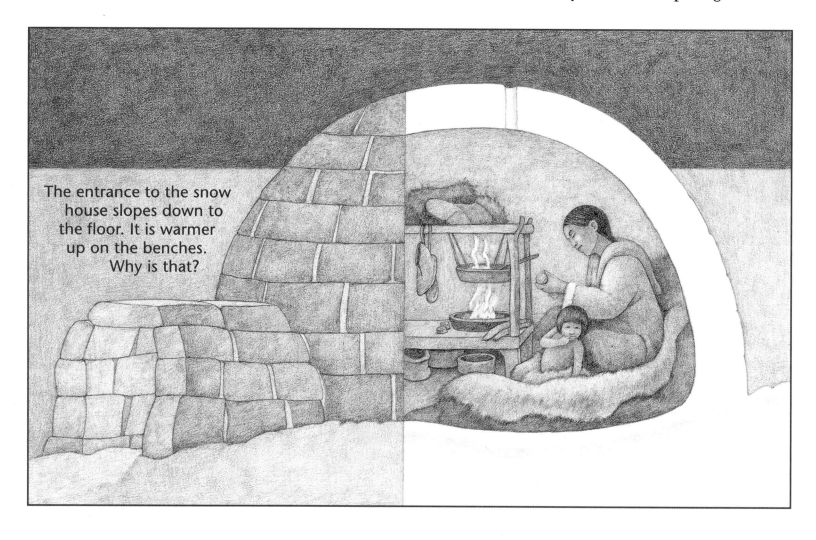

The entrance to the snow house slopes down to the floor. It is warmer up on the benches. Why is that?

REAL PEOPLE: IKPAKHUAK and HIGILAK

It's because of Ikpakhuak [eck-PAHK-hoo-ahk] and Higilak [HEE-gee-lahk] that we know as much as we do about the traditional life of the Copper Inuit. From 1914 to 1916, there was an expedition to the Copper Inuit lands to record information about traditional culture. Ikpakhuak was a respected hunter. Ikpakhuak and his wife Higilak adopted a member of the expedition and taught him about their culture. The people on the expedition wrote down what they saw and took photos.

Keeping the Lamp Burning

Oil-burning lamps provided warmth and light inside the igloos. The lamps didn't get hot enough to melt the snow houses, though! Lamps were also used for cooking.

Keeping the seal-oil lamp burning was an important job for women. Seal blubber was crushed to create the oil. As it melted, it burned. Lamps came in all sizes, from about 5 centimetres to 1 metre.

In winter, the most common meal for the Copper Inuit was boiled seal meat. A woman melted some snow in a soapstone dish over the fire, then added the meat. For extra flavour, seal blood or blubber was added.

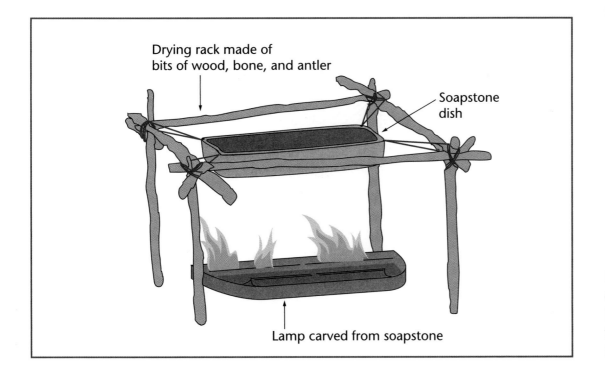

Drying rack made of bits of wood, bone, and antler

Soapstone dish

Lamp carved from soapstone

Lamps were too heavy to carry on summer trips. Instead, people used tundra plants such as heather to make small fires.

A Closer Look

Cooking and Keeping Food

All Aboriginal communities relied on two important technologies for survival. One was fire for warmth and cooking. The other was drying food to keep for times when there was no harvesting or hunting.

Fire

Fires were started by lighting a spark to tinder. (Tinder is bits of dry wood or plants that easily catch fire.) A spark was made by striking two stones together or by rubbing a stick quickly against a piece of wood. The spark then caused the tinder to catch fire.

Drying Food

Meat, fish, and berries keep a long time if they are dried while they're still fresh. Meat was thinly sliced, while fish was usually split in half. Berries were mashed or left whole. The food was then spread on racks or hung on poles or lines to dry. In dry climates, this was often done outdoors. In wetter areas, drying took place indoors.

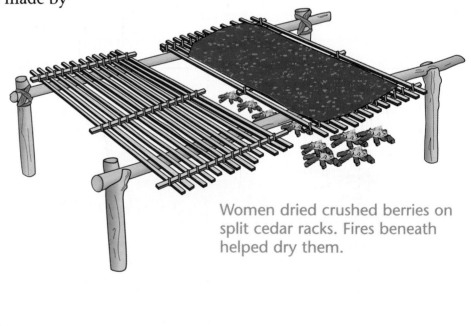

Women dried crushed berries on split cedar racks. Fires beneath helped dry them.

Inuit Art

In the past, Inuit men carved patterns or pictures on everyday objects such as needle cases and knives. Inuit women created designs on hides when they made clothing. (Copper Inuit women made especially beautiful clothing.) Today, Inuit artists are famous all over the world for their carvings and other forms of art, such as pictures made from pieces of fabric and prints made on paper.

This picture is by Kingmeata Etidlooie [king-mee-A-ta ay-TID-loo-ee], a modern artist from Cape Dorset in the eastern part of the Arctic. The picture is called "Summer Camp Scene." How can you tell that this picture doesn't show a Copper Inuit fishing camp?

Try This

Make a picture in the style of Kingmeata Etidlooie that shows a Copper Inuit family in their summer or winter camp. Include details that show how they used the natural resources in their environment to meet their basic needs.

You'll have to skim this section and the section called "The Copper Inuit" on pages 51 to 56 to find the information you need to create your picture.

DANCING TO THE DRUM

There is more to culture than meeting basic needs. People also have to figure out how to get along, raise their children, and decide what things they believe in. They also have to find time to have fun!

People wore specially decorated clothing for Drum Dances. These were lighter than their other clothing. How do you think Drum Dancing helped people get along?

Government

In traditional Copper Inuit communities, the husband and wife and their children lived and worked together. Other relatives lived with the family from time to time. Men usually had a partner for hunting. This was an important relationship, and it usually lasted for life.

The Copper Inuit had no leaders or chiefs. Decisions were usually made by the entire group. Sometimes, though, the best hunters had a greater say.

The Drum Dance was the Copper Inuit's main form of celebration. Drum Dances were held any time, but they were a common way to welcome visitors. In winter, people living in large groups joined their igloos to a central igloo. This is where the Drum Dancing was held. Anyone could lead a dance and sing a song. The others joined in. People who made up good songs were very popular.

Growing Up

Copper Inuit children stayed close to their mothers until they were three or four years old. They were carried inside their mother's coat. A hood on a mother's coat was large enough for a child's head, too. Girls would often carry puppies in their hoods!

Whenever a hunter made a kill, the food was shared with others. There were traditions about who got which part of the animal. It was the woman's job to butcher the animal and give out the food.

Today, most Inuit live in towns, and children go to school. Many families still hunt on weekends and during holidays, though. Because communities are small and far apart, Inuit students often use modern technology like the Internet to keep in touch with each other.

Think For Yourself

Discuss one of these topics in a group, then give your opinion.

- *Do groups make better decisions if they have one leader or if everyone has a say?*
- *What is the best way to teach children how to get along with others?*

Ask for someone in your group to volunteer to present your group's ideas to the class. Don't forget to support your opinion with facts and examples. Describe any differences of opinion your group had.

It was considered wrong to cause unnecessary pain to an animal, and no part of an animal was ever wasted. Responsible hunting practices are still important to the Inuit today.

Most Aboriginal groups had shamans as spiritual leaders. In some groups, shamans could be men or women. In many groups, though, only a man could be a shaman.

The children were never punished. Adults believed that punishment damaged a child's spirit. Children learned what they needed to know and how to behave by watching their parents.

Everyone in a community had to work hard to survive. Boys and girls helped drive the caribou during the summer hunts. Boys learned how to hunt by trapping birds and small animals during the summer. As soon as they were strong enough, they began hunting seals and caribou with the men.

Girls learned to sew and cook by helping their mothers. They also trapped birds and small animals and collected berries and eggs during the summer.

Beliefs

All Inuit believed in a world in which spirits had various powers that could harm or help people. The most powerful spirit was a woman who lived at the bottom of the sea.

In daily life, it was important to honour these spirits by showing respect for animals that were killed in the hunt. For example, people believed that creatures that lived in the sea were thirsty from the salt water. So when a seal was killed, fresh water was poured into its mouth as a way of showing respect.

A **shaman** [SHAY-mun] was a person with a special connection to the spirit world. Some illnesses were believed to be caused by spirits. So a shaman was called upon to help drive out the harmful spirit. A shaman also contributed to important decisions made by the group.

In The Words Of...

The Elders

Many Inuit believed that the spirits or souls of the dead came back in people who were named after them. They also believed that animals sometimes offered themselves to be killed to suit their own purposes or to help people.

In this story, a man's soul travels through many creatures before it is born again. This story has been passed on for many years in Inuit communities.

The hunter Mako [MAH-koe] chases a fox-woman into the hills and falls asleep in her burrow. This story starts when Mako awakens, many months later.

When he awoke, there was a humming of flies around the entrance to the burrow and it was full summer. He walked outside, and there were grass and flowers. But now he was no longer a man. He was a spirit.

"What form shall I choose for my soul to wander in?" he asked himself. Then he crept into a blade of grass.

For a short time he remained in peace. But when the wind stirred, he swayed back and forth, and soon he became tired of the constant motion. Then he crept into the body of a raven.

Ravens never go hungry, as it seemed to him, but they often feel cold around their feet. And so he stopped being a raven and became a caribou.

He joined a herd of caribou, and they all moved off together. In their wanderings Mako was always behind the others. They asked him, "Why are you so slow?"

He answered, "I keep stumbling all the time." Then they told him how to look at the stars as he walked along. "Watching the ground makes you stumble," they said. After this, he followed their advice and was able to keep up with them.

"What shall I eat?" he asked.

"Scratch away the snow with your forefeet and find moss," they answered. Then he ate moss and grew fat.

One day the herd was attacked by a wolf, and all the caribou dashed into the sea. Mako ran with them, and when he reached the water his soul crept into a walrus. He became hungry. He went down to the bottom of the sea to dig clams. But the clams would not open their shells, and he came up still hungry.

He said to the other walruses, "I can't get anything to eat. The clams refuse to open their shells for me."

The other walruses said, "When you get down to the bottom of the sea, say yock-yock-yock!" Then he went back to the bottom and said yock! The clams opened their shells, and he had all he wanted to eat. The others ate too.

After the walruses had eaten their fill, they climbed onto the rocks to rest. Mako went with them. Soon the others returned to the water, but Mako was tired of being a walrus, and he said to himself, "Now what form shall I choose for my soul to wander in?"

Just then a seal swam by, and Mako crept into it. For a long time he lived among the seals. One day, however, he looked to the shore and saw houses, and in one of the houses nearest the shore lived a woman who had not yet had a child.

Mako lay in wait for that woman's husband. One day he came up to breathe just in front of the place where the man was standing. The man harpooned him, and when he felt himself struck, he almost laughed aloud.

Now he was hauled ashore and brought into the house. They began to cut him up, and when the man threw his mittens to his wife, Mako went with the mittens and crept into the body of the woman. After a time he was born again as the woman's child.

Then they had to find a name for him, and at first they called him after a dead relative. They did not call him Mako. And hearing a strange name, he began to cry.

One day this father, who was very fond of him and looked after him, heard him saying, "I am Mako." The father was so astonished that he nearly dropped him. "Ha!" said the father. "He wants to be named after that Mako who was lost in the hills. He is Mako!"

Then the child stopped crying and entered upon his human life once again. When he had grown to be an old man, it became a story. And those who came after him constantly told it further.

Now it is finished. I don't know any more.

From *The Dancing Fox: Arctic Folktales*, edited by John Bierhorst (New York: William Morrow & Company, 1997), pp. 117-120.

Try This

Decide on a way to share Mako's story with others. You might want to read the story in a group, act out the story, draw a picture of one part of the story, or make up a song about Mako that you can sing with a drum.

Looking Back

In this chapter, you found out about the traditional culture of the Copper Inuit.

What have you learned that might help you to investigate the traditional cultures of other Aboriginal groups in Canada?

Where Cedars Meet the Sea

The province of British Columbia includes three of Canada's regions: the West Coast, the Subarctic, and the Plateau. Within these regions, there is a rich heritage of many different Aboriginal cultures.

In this chapter, you can look at traditional Aboriginal territories in all of British Columbia. Then you can find out about the people whose traditional territories are in the coastal region of the province.

If you live in the coastal region, the technology, government, beliefs, and art described in this chapter might include things you see or do in your community every day.

Traditional Territories

Who are the Aboriginal peoples of British Columbia?

The map on page 69 shows the groups that Aboriginal peoples in British Columbia have formed today. Each group includes people from many communities. The people in each group have **similar** cultures and speak similar languages. Together, they claim the areas shown on the map as their **traditional territories**.

There are no exact borders for the traditional territories because people moved around over time. Not everyone agrees where one territory ends and another one begins.

Things that are similar are alike, but not exactly the same.

Try This

Which traditional Aboriginal territory is your community in? Which territories are nearby?

What We Call This Place

The names of places on modern maps are the names Europeans gave these places when they came to North America. Of course, Aboriginal peoples already had names for these places. In the past, Aboriginal peoples did not write down their languages and they didn't make maps. Instead, Elders taught the names to younger people.

Sometimes European mapmakers tried to write down the Aboriginal names for places. They didn't always get them right, though. This was because they didn't know how to speak Aboriginal languages. You might have the same problem if you tried to write down a word from a language that you don't speak.

The place names that are in red on the map are the Aboriginal names for these places. These are only a few examples. There are many more Aboriginal place names in British Columbia.

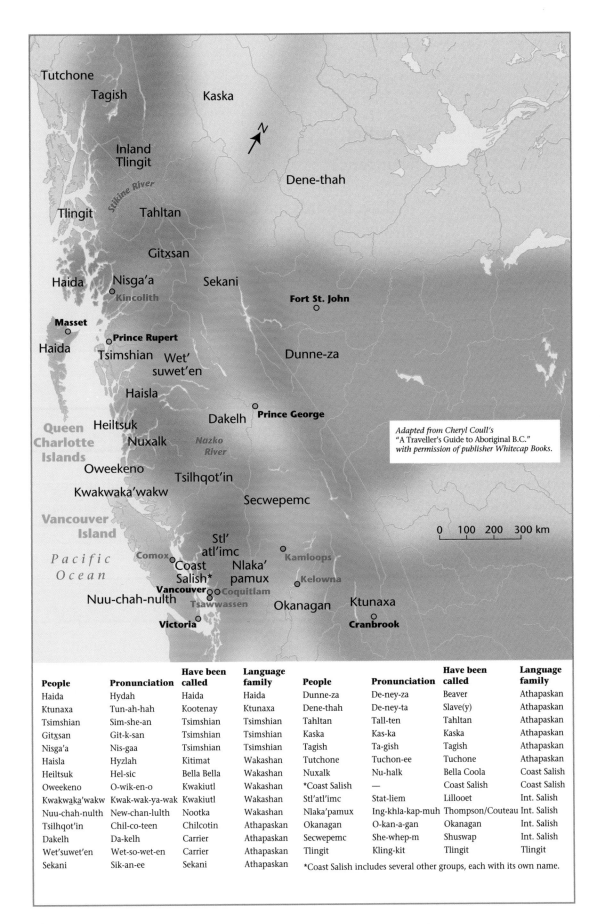

This map shows the traditional territories of Aboriginal peoples in BC. Take your time reading it—it includes a lot of information. To find out the meaning of the Aboriginal names in red, see "What's in a Name?" on page 70.

Adapted from Cheryl Coull's "A Traveller's Guide to Aboriginal B.C." with permission of publisher Whitecap Books.

Many Aboriginal groups have two names. This is because they were once known by the name Europeans called them. Today, they prefer to be known by their own names in their own languages. With a partner, practice saying the names of the different groups. Are any names familiar to you?

People	Pronunciation	Have been called	Language family	People	Pronunciation	Have been called	Language family
Haida	Hydah	Haida	Haida	Dunne-za	De-ney-za	Beaver	Athapaskan
Ktunaxa	Tun-ah-hah	Kootenay	Ktunaxa	Dene-thah	De-ney-ta	Slave(y)	Athapaskan
Tsimshian	Sim-she-an	Tsimshian	Tsimshian	Tahltan	Tall-ten	Tahltan	Athapaskan
Gitxsan	Git-k-san	Tsimshian	Tsimshian	Kaska	Kas-ka	Kaska	Athapaskan
Nisga'a	Nis-gaa	Tsimshian	Tsimshian	Tagish	Ta-gish	Tagish	Athapaskan
Haisla	Hyzlah	Kitimat	Wakashan	Tutchone	Tuchon-ee	Tuchone	Athapaskan
Heiltsuk	Hel-sic	Bella Bella	Wakashan	Nuxalk	Nu-halk	Bella Coola	Coast Salish
Oweekeno	O-wik-en-o	Kwakiutl	Wakashan	*Coast Salish	—	Coast Salish	Coast Salish
Kwakwaka'wakw	Kwak-wak-ya-wak	Kwakiutl	Wakashan	Stl'atl'imc	Stat-liem	Lillooet	Int. Salish
Nuu-chah-nulth	New-chan-lulth	Nootka	Wakashan	Nlaka'pamux	Ing-khla-kap-muh	Thompson/Couteau	Int. Salish
Tsilhqot'in	Chil-co-teen	Chilcotin	Athapaskan	Okanagan	O-kan-a-gan	Okanagan	Int. Salish
Dakelh	Da-kelh	Carrier	Athapaskan	Secwepemc	She-whep-m	Shuswap	Int. Salish
Wet'suwet'en	Wet-so-wet-en	Carrier	Athapaskan	Tlingit	Kling-kit	Tlingit	Tlingit
Sekani	Sik-an-ee	Sekani	Athapaskan				

*Coast Salish includes several other groups, each with its own name.

What's in a Name?

Place Name	Meaning	Language Family
Comox	"abundance"	Wakashan
Coquitlam	"smell like fish"	Coast Salish
Tsawwassen	"looking towards the sea"	Coast Salish
Kelowna	"grizzly bear"	Interior Salish
Kamloops	"where the rivers meet"	Interior Salish
Nazko	"river flowing from the south"	Athapaskan
Kincolith	"place of skulls"	Tsimshian
Stikine	"great river"	Athapaskan

Think For Yourself

Look at the box called "What's in a Name?" In a group, discuss what these names tell you about the history and the environment of British Columbia.

Find Out

Find out the Aboriginal names for one or two places in your community.

You might find that some place names are based on Aboriginal names, like the ones in "What's in a Name?" You might find that a place known by one name today has an older name that some Aboriginal people remember. Record the names and the history they tell you.

Before you start, brainstorm some sources of information about Aboriginal names. You might want to work in a group. Each group member could then try a different source of information.

Coastal Communities

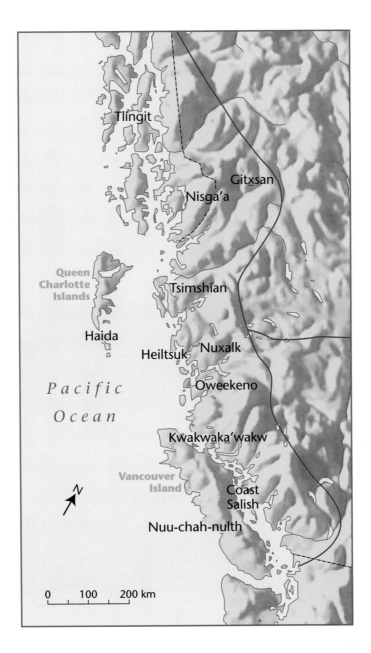

A long the coast of British Columbia, thick coniferous forests meet the waters of the Pacific Ocean. Many rivers flow from the forest into the sea. There are both rocky shores and sandy beaches.

This mix of environments creates a region that is rich in natural resources. The ocean and forests provide a variety of foods, as well as materials for clothing, transportation, and shelter. The climate is also easy to live in—it's never very hot or very cold. You do have to get used to a lot of rain, though!

You can see from the map on this page that several different Aboriginal groups have

Coastal forests are thick, with many smaller plants growing beneath the large trees. Some coastal trees can grow as tall as 60 metres and be 2.5 metres across at the trunk.

This map shows the coastal region of British Columbia. Where are mountains located? How would you describe the **coastline** (where the ocean meets the shore)?

Tlingit

Gitxsan

Nisga'a

Queen
Charlotte
Islands

Tsimshian

Haida

Heiltsuk Nuxalk

Pacific

Ocean

Oweekeno

Kwakwaka'wakw

Vancouver
Island

Coast
Salish

Nuu-chah-nulth

0   100   200 km

traditional territories in the coastal region of British Columbia. As you read about traditional life here, you'll see that these groups had many things in common. You'll also discover that each culture was special in many ways, too.

Villages were usually located along the seashore near a river. Sometimes they were located along the side of a river.

Villages

Coastal peoples lived in villages. A small village had two or three houses. A larger village had as many as 15 or 20 houses. These villages were the coastal peoples' main homes.

In most villages, people travelled in spring, summer, and autumn to find good fishing spots or to gather berries, roots, and shellfish. They didn't need to go far. They brought all the food they collected back to their village to store for the winter.

This is a drawing of a Haida [HY-duh] village. What can you tell about life in the village from this picture? Why do you think it was important to live near the water?

Really Big Houses!

Almost all coastal houses were built from cedar wood. These houses were called **longhouses** or **bighouses**. Houses were given names, such as "People Wish to Be Here" and "Grease House." The names told people something about the house.

Several related families lived together in one house. This might include anywhere from 20 to 80 people. Woven mats or wooden panels separated each family's living space. Some houses had a central fire pit that everyone used for cooking and heat. In other houses, each family had its own fire pit.

The house was also the storage place for all the food and other goods the family used during the year. Dried food, cedar bark, and other items were hung from the ceiling or stored in large boxes or baskets. Sometimes there were wide shelves along the walls for storing things.

Today, many Aboriginal communities have a bighouse or longhouse where special ceremonies and celebrations take place.

These are three different styles of houses people built on the coast. What is the same about these houses? What's different? What do you think each house was like inside?

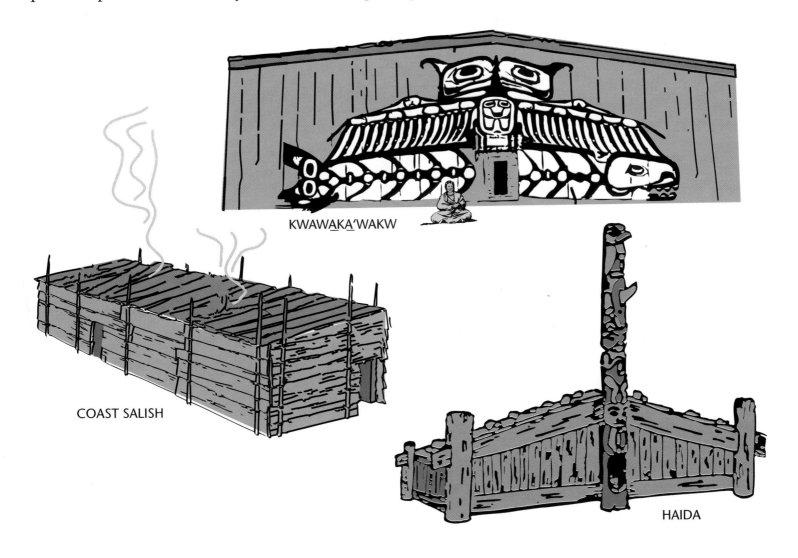

KWAWAKA'WAKW

COAST SALISH

HAIDA

A Closer Look

Crests

The traditional art of coastal peoples most often displayed the family's **crests**. A crest is a drawing or carving that tells the story of a time when the family gave or got help from a spirit in animal form. The crest shows a creature from the story.

The painting on the front of the Kwakwaka'wakw [kwah-KWAH-kah-wahkw] house on page 73 shows Thunderbird catching a whale. Thunderbird is a very powerful crest, which tells you that this house belongs to an important chief. Can you see the whale?

Totem poles are tall carvings that are made up of many crests, one on top of the other. Many communities placed totem poles near their houses or built them as part of the house.

The Haida house on page 73 has a **frontal pole** attached to it. (See if you can pick out the separate crests.)

The Coast Salish [KOHST SAY-lish] are the only coastal peoples who do not have the tradition of displaying crests.

This is a bear crest from a Tlingit drum.

This is a kwakwaka'wakw feast dish with a wolf crest. It is about 3 m long!

Canoes

During spring, summer, and autumn, coastal peoples travelled a lot. They made trips to fish or gather food, to trade, to visit family, and to raid their enemies. Canoes were their main form of transportation. The thick forests, steep hills, and jagged coastline made it difficult to travel by land.

A coastal canoe was carved out of one cedar log. Long, deep canoes were used for ocean travel. Curved fronts and backs were often added on to the main canoe. A big ocean-going canoe held as many as 40 people.

Both men and women paddled the ocean canoes. On long voyages, a drummer helped to keep the beat while the people sang paddle songs.

All coastal peoples used shorter, shallow canoes for river travel. These canoes held about four people. Poles were often used to push along a river canoe.

Every community had simple canoes for work such as fishing and carved and painted larger canoes for special celebrations and war.

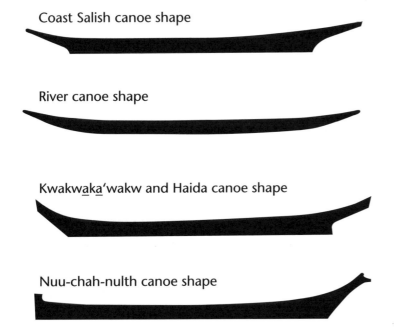

Coast Salish canoe shape

River canoe shape

Kwakwaka'wakw and Haida canoe shape

Nuu-chah-nulth canoe shape

Haida ceremonial canoe

The Haida and the Nuu-chah-nulth [noo-CHAH-noolth] were especially famous for the sturdy canoes they made. Their territories had the right climate to grow very large cedar trees.

Try This

Draw a picture of a small coastal community—just two or three houses. You could draw a Haida, Kwakwaka'wakw, or Coast Salish community. Make your houses and your canoes the right style for your community. You might want to name your houses. Don't forget to show the environment!

A Closer Look

Working with Wood

Coastal peoples used cedar to make many things—houses, paddles, canoes, dishes, totem poles, and masks.

Cedar is valuable because it has oils that keep it from rotting. It also splits easily, is easy to carve, and is light to carry!

To fell a tree, a man would use an **adze** [ADZ] to make a small hole in the side. (An adze is like an axe made with a stone blade.) The hole was then filled with hot rocks, which made the wood burn a little. Then it could be chipped away more easily. Fallen trees were split into long boards called **planks**.

To split the planks from the trunk, wedges were pounded into the wood with a **maul** [MAHL]. (A maul works like a hammer.) Often a few planks were cut from a living tree. (This didn't harm the tree, though.)

Aboriginal peoples didn't have nails. Sometimes planks were tied in place using long, thin strands of cedar bows.

Food and Clothing

In coastal communities, most of the gathering and **preserving** of food took place in spring, summer, and autumn. Winter was a quieter time. For most Aboriginal groups, this was the time for many special ceremonies.

Each community had a different **seasonal cycle**. The cycle depended on the resources in the area. The chart shows the seasonal cycle in a Tsimshian [TSIM-shee-un] community.

For most coastal communities, hunting was a small part of their

Preserving food made sure that it kept for a long time. Then it could be eaten later when fresh food wasn't available.

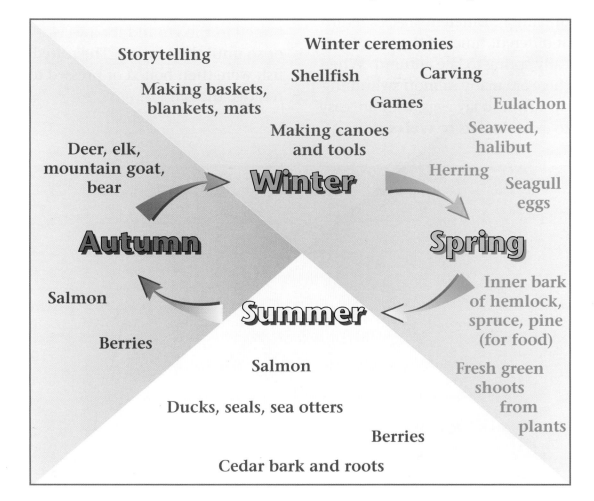

Storytelling

Winter ceremonies

Shellfish   Carving

Making baskets, blankets, mats

Games

Eulachon

Making canoes and tools

Seaweed, halibut

Deer, elk, mountain goat, bear

Herring

Winter

Seagull eggs

Autumn   **Spring**

Salmon

Inner bark of hemlock, spruce, pine (for food)

Summer

Berries

Fresh green shoots from plants

Salmon

Ducks, seals, sea otters

Berries

Cedar bark and roots

The Tsimshian had winter homes by the ocean. In the spring, they moved to **eulachon** sites to fish. In the summer, they fished at salmon sites. In the autumn, they moved to the hunting grounds. All of these places were close to their winter homes.

Coastal people made many different types of fishing gear.

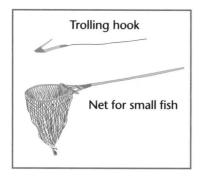
Trolling hook

Net for small fish

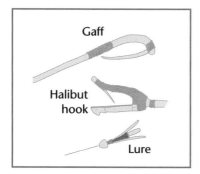
Gaff

Halibut hook

Lure

This is a Coast Salish salmon weir. The salmon swim into the fence made of sticks and get trapped. They are then easily scooped up. Why do you think fishers sometimes opened the weir so that some salmon were able to get through?

seasonal cycle. Resources from the ocean were plentiful and easier to catch than forest animals. Men did most of the fishing. Women collected shellfish from the shore and gathered berries and other plants from the forest.

Salmon

Salmon was the main source of food for most communities. Salmon is a valuable resource because the fish return to the same rivers to lay their eggs at the same time each year. So coastal peoples always knew when and where to find food!

There are five **species**, or kinds, of salmon. Different species return at different times of the year, from early spring to late autumn. When there are many salmon swimming up a river to lay eggs, they are easy to catch in nets or **weirs**.

Eulachon

Eulachon are small, slow-swimming fish. In late April or early May, they come to the rivers by the thousands to lay their eggs. This was the best time for coastal peoples to fish for eulachon.

Some eulachon were dried or smoked and used as food. But the most important reason for catching eulachon was for their oil. This was a good source of vitamins and it was added to all kinds of food, from smoked salmon to dried berries!

The fish were caught in traps or scooped up in nets. Back on shore, they were put in tubs or buried in the ground for a week or so until they rotted. The rotted fish were then boiled or pressed to remove the oil.

Eulachon oil was a valuable item. It was traded to people along the coast who didn't live near a river with a eulachon run and to people who lived in the Interior away from the coast. People still fish for eulachon today.

Other Food from the Sea

Coastal peoples caught other kinds of fish, such as herring, halibut, and cod. In the Haida and Tlingit [TLING-it] territories, there wasn't as much salmon as there was in other places, so these people ate more halibut.

Clams, mussels, oysters, and sea urchins were some of the shellfish people enjoyed. They also ate certain kinds of seaweed.

Coastal peoples also hunted sea mammals, such as otters, seals, and porpoises. Whale meat and blubber were valued, but most people didn't hunt whales. Instead, they waited for a whale to wash up on shore naturally. This sometimes happened if a whale swam into shallow waters. Coastal peoples sang special songs to encourage the whales to swim closer to shore.

Only the Nuu-chah-nulth went to sea to hunt whales.

More Food

Coastal peoples also gathered a variety of plants, roots, bulbs, and berries. As they picked, they sang special songs of thanks to these forest resources.

At certain times of the year, ducks and geese were on the menu. Coastal peoples also collected duck and seagull eggs. They always made sure that they left at least one egg for the mother bird to hatch, though. Why do you think they did this?

Some plants were also gathered to be used as medicine.

Agnes Edgar

Raven is an important figure in many coastal stories. When he wanted to, Raven could change himself from human to bird form. He was good at tricking people and other animals. He sometimes caused problems for people, but he often helped out, too.

In this story, Agnes Edgar, a Nuxalk Elder, tells how Raven brought soapberries to the Bella Coola Valley.

Soapberries were soaked in water and then whipped until they were frothy. Flavoured with eulachon oil, this was a favourite dessert in all parts of British Columbia.

Well, I'll tell you now about the story about the woman named Simlayxana [seem-ly-ZAH-nuh] who was dropped down here at the head of the valley. She came down [from the Land Above]…with soapberries so she would have a means of surviving. After she was here awhile she was approached by someone she took to be a human being. He wanted to make friends with her, but she didn't want to share her soapberries—her food—with anyone so she tried to keep to herself. After awhile, however, she took some soapberries from her stores and gave them to the one she thought was a man to soak. He took them and told her he would whip them up as well.

Now the one she thought was a man was really Raven. He came to make friends with Simlayxana just because of the soapberries. We wouldn't have soapberries here in the Bella Coola Valley today if it wasn't for Raven. He made friends with her just to get ahold of some soapberries.

Taking some soapberries for himself, Raven started to walk from the head of the valley towards the mouth of the river. He carried the soapberries in his beak while at the same time making his "caw-caw" sound as he walked. This way he scattered the soapberries from the head of the valley to the mouth of the river. And from these soapberries he dropped come all the soapberries we now have in the valley.

Raven

From Ruth Kirk, *Wisdom of the Elders: Native Traditions on the Northwest Coast* (Vancouver: Douglas & McIntyre). Copyright British Columbia Provincial Museum, 1986.

Preparing the Catch

When foods were in season, people ate them fresh. Grilled fish, steamed clams, and ripe berries made delicious meals. The fish was skewered on a stick and grilled over a small fire. Clams were steamed open under a covering of damp seaweed.

While they were enjoying fresh food, however, the women also prepared food to keep for winter. Fish, berries, roots, clams, and seaweed were dried and stored in boxes and baskets.

Fish was sometimes smoked as well. When it came time to eat it, the fish was dipped in seal, whale, or eulachon oil to soften it.

Sometimes fish was boiled in water to make soup. To heat the water, the cook placed rocks in a fire. When the rocks were red hot, they were removed with a stick and placed into a cedar box filled with water. When the rocks cooled, they were taken out and replaced with more hot rocks. After awhile, a piping hot soup was ready to eat!

At meals, food was served on large wooden platters set in the centre of the group. Each person had a spoon carved out of wood. Napkins were made of shredded cedar bark that had been pounded until it was soft.

This drawing was made by one of the first Europeans to visit a Nuu-chah-nulth house. What do you think is hanging from the ceiling to dry? What is the woman doing with the rocks?

A Closer Look

Gathering

Women and girls gathered berries, roots, and plants from the forest and carried them in baskets. Most baskets and straps were made of cedar. The strap used for carrying heavy baskets is called a **tumpline**.

How do you think girls learned which berries to pick?

Why do you think the tumpline is thicker across the front?

Everyday Clothing

What have you noticed about the clothing in the pictures you've seen of coastal life in this chapter?

You might have noticed that people wore woven clothing. For all coastal peoples, everyday clothing was usually made from the soft inner bark of the cedar tree. The bark was peeled off in strips and pounded to make soft strands for weaving. Woven cedar-bark clothing was waterproof and warm enough for the coastal climate.

West Coast peoples did not wear shoes. This made it easier to climb in and out of canoes and to explore the seashore looking for shellfish.

Special Robes

Coast Salish women wove blankets out of the wool from mountain goats or the hair of special dogs they kept for this purpose. The blankets the women of the Chilkat [CHIL-kat] community (Tlingit territory) wove displayed family crests.

Blankets weren't used on beds. They were worn as robes by important people on special occasions. Blankets were valuable trade items along the coast.

Important people also wore furs. The fur of sea otters was especially valued.

This is a painting by an early European visitor to a Coast Salish house. Notice the woman in the background spinning the yarn. What parts of this picture seem to be based on the artist's own culture rather than traditional Coast Salish culture?

Try This

Make an oral presentation on one of these main ideas:
- The cedar tree was an important natural resource for coastal peoples.
- The ocean was an important natural resource for coastal peoples.

In your presentation, include two or three facts or examples of resources and how they were used. (Remember, an oral presentation begins with your main idea, then gives the facts and examples. It finishes by reminding people about your main idea.)

You can find the facts and examples you need by skimming this section and the section called "Coastal Communities" on pages 71 to 76. You might want to use a chart like this to record the information you find.

MAIN IDEA: The cedar tree was was an important natural resource for coastal peoples.

Details
- Houses were made from cedar

Spirits and Ceremonies

In traditional coastal cultures, there was a strong connection between beliefs, government, and art.

Beliefs

In coastal cultures, there are many stories that tell of spirits taking different human or animal forms. You've already read about Raven. Salmon People and Bear People are two other types of animal spirits.

People showed respect for the spirits by not taking more resources than they needed and by sharing what they took with others. Learning the special ceremonies and the ways of showing respect for nature were important lessons for Aboriginal children.

People hoped that at some time in their life they would get a **spirit helper**. This is a spirit that would help them through life. A spirit helper might show itself to the person in a dream or after a long period of time spent alone.

Do you remember the ceremony the Stó:lō had to show respect for the Salmon People? This First Salmon ceremony was celebrated in many coastal communities.

Winter ceremonies that included dances, songs, and stories were one way people showed their beliefs. Ceremonies often included costumes, masks, whistles, and rattles. This photograph of Nuxalk dancers was taken in 1886. The patterned blankets are Chilkat blankets.

Peter Webster

Nuu-chah-nulth Elder Peter Webster tells about the respect his father had for the spirit of the cedar trees.

I remember watching my father cut down a cedar tree from which he was going to make a large dugout canoe. He carried out his work with great respect for the tree. He would talk to it as though to a fellow human being. He would ask the tree not to hurt him, as he was going to change it into a beautiful object that was to be useful to him.

From Ruth Kirk, *Wisdom of the Elders: Native Traditions on the Northwest Coast* (Vancouver: Douglas & McIntyre). Copyright British Columbia Provincial Museum, 1986.

Kin is another word for *relative*. Sometimes kin groups were also called **clans**.

Government

The most important connection for people in coastal communities was to the house they lived in. Everyone in the house was related in some way.

The mask on the cover of this book was carved by a Haisla [HY-sluh] artist named Lyle Wilson. He created this piece of art as a sign of respect for the Eagle, an ancestral bird of his clan.

Several related houses belonged to a **kin group**. A kin group could include several communities. People in the same kin group shared a relative in the past. Kin groups usually had the names of animals that were important in their history, such as Eagle, Raven, Wolf, or Beaver.

Honours and Goods

In coastal communities, people kept track of who had the rights to **honours** (such as crests, songs, and ceremonies) and **goods** (such as berry patches and fishing grounds). They did this by giving ancestral names to members of their family.

In The Words Of...

Lyle Wilson

Lyle Wilson grew up watching his uncle Sam Robinson carve, and he studied art at college and university. Here's what he says about the mask on the cover of this book.

The Eagle is an ancestral bird of my clan. The Eagle represents the universal characteristics of pride, beauty, and ferociousness.

This mask was inspired by the sheer beauty of this great bird and my own observations of it, as well as by an older mask of a clan chief, Sunahead, which is the mask of the highest-ranking chief of the Eagle clan. I refused to use real eagle feathers because it would mean the death of an eagle. I chose to carve feathers out of yellow cedar.

From Gary Wyatt, *Spirit Faces: Contemporary Masks of the Northwest Coast* (Vancouver: Douglas and McIntyre) Copyright © 1994 by the Inuit Gallery.

Ancestral names were given at large gatherings called **potlatches**. At a potlatch, there was plenty of good food and lots of singing, dancing, and storytelling. The celebration usually lasted for several days.

The people who were invited to the potlatch were asked to **witness**. This meant that they were asked to remember who had been given the name and what honours and goods went with it. This was a good way of keeping records in a culture that didn't write things down.

The family that held the potlatch gave many gifts to all the witnesses. They might even give away everything they had. Families who gave away their goods were admired. Another time, they would be invited to a potlatch. Then they would be the ones to receive gifts.

Being Worthy
A person only received an ancestral name when she or he proved to be **worthy**. A worthy person knew and respected all the cultural traditions and was generous towards others. A very worthy person had many ancestral names, which meant lots of honours and goods!

Chiefs
In the past, all chiefs came from **noble** families. Noble families have many ancestral rights. A chief was usually the oldest male in the family, but in some groups women could be chiefs.

Potlatches or feasts were held to mark all important events in life, such as birth, becoming an adult, marriage, and death. Potlatches are still an important tradition for many families today.

Today, many Aboriginal communities have two kinds of chiefs: hereditary chiefs (with ancestral rights) and chiefs elected by the community.

All the chiefs in a village had their **rank** (position compared to others). When an important decision had to be made, all the chiefs got together to discuss the matter.

Usually, each chief had his own house. The other families in the house were related to the chief in some way. The other families did not have ancestral rights, so they helped the chief to hunt, fish, gather, and preserve the resources that were part of his rights. The chief couldn't do it all by himself.

The families also worked together to perform special ceremonies. People would be related to many different chiefs. So if a chief was not wise and fair, people could leave the house and live with another chief.

Some chiefs owned **slaves**. Slaves were usually people taken prisoner in raids. They had no rights or family connections. They lived in the house with family members.

REAL PEOPLE: CHIEF MUNGO MARTIN (c.1881 – 1965)

Mungo Martin's first Kwakwa̱ka'wakw name was Kisuyakilis [kee-soo-yuh-KEE-lis]—"Coming-Out-to-Do-Something-for-Everyone." During his life, he was given eight additional names with many honours.

Mungo Martin was an expert carver. All his life he worked to fix old totem poles and to make new ones. He shared his knowledge of carving with others. He recorded his memories on tape to make sure that everything he knew about traditional Kwakwa̱ka'wakw culture would be remembered for the future.

Think For Yourself

In a group, discuss these two questions. The first question is an inquiry that asks you to think of facts and examples. The second question asks you to give your opinion.

- *How did coastal peoples use art in their daily lives, beliefs, and government?*
- *Do you think it is important for Aboriginal peoples today to work in their traditional art forms?*

You might want to put on a display about Aboriginal art, past and present, to help others in your school learn more about it.

Find Out

Pick one coastal group and do a research project to find out more about its culture. You might want to find out about how things were in the past. Or you might be more interested in what is happening today.

You could present the results of your research in a model, a wall mural, or a story.

HOW TO... Use Key Words in Research

Key words can help you find information in the library or on the Internet. (Remember, a key word is the name of a person, group, place, or thing or an important word from the question you are investigating.)

1. In the library, use key words to look up subjects in the catalogue of books.

2. On the Internet, use key words for your searches.

Looking Back

In this chapter, you learned about the traditional cultures of Aboriginal peoples in coastal British Columbia. You also discovered that traditions are still important today.

What do you think is the most important BIG QUESTION to ask when you are investigating a culture?

Chapter 6

Into the Interior

How can dreaming help a hunter find animals? What do beaver tracks look like? How could you make a home underground? In this chapter, you can investigate the traditional Aboriginal cultures of the Interior and find answers to these questions.

The Interior of British Columbia is made up of two regions: the Subarctic in the north and the Plateau in the south. For Aboriginal peoples in the past, the main difference between these two regions was in the type of resources that were available.

As you learn about traditional Interior cultures, think about how they are the same as or different from other Aboriginal cultures you know about.

Interior Environments

The Subarctic Region

There are a lot of mountains in the Subarctic region. The main vegetation is coniferous forest of spruce and pine. But there are also **deciduous** trees such as poplar, birch, and willow.

There are many lakes and rivers in the Subarctic. There are also large areas of swampy soil called **muskeg**.

Subarctic Peoples

Many Aboriginal peoples in the Subarctic region traditionally depended on **game** to meet their basic needs. When hunting went well, they dried and stored meat to eat in winter. This wasn't enough to last throughout the long winters, though, so Subarctic peoples hunted year round.

Deciduous trees lose their leaves in winter.

Game is wild animals and birds that are hunted for food.

Moose live throughout the Interior. They especially like to eat the willow trees and water plants found in the wet areas of the Subarctic. Moose can dive under water to get plants to eat!

This map shows the Subarctic and Plateau regions of the Interior of British Columbia.

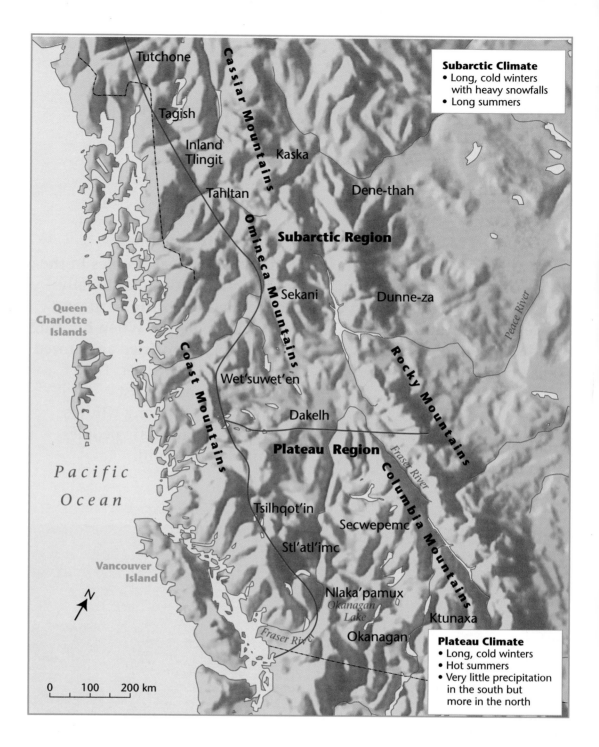

Tutchone

Cassiar Mountains

Tagish

Inland Tlingit

Kaska

Tahltan

Dene-thah

Subarctic Climate
• Long, cold winters with heavy snowfalls
• Long summers

Subarctic Region

Omineca Mountains

Sekani

Dunne-za

Peace River

Queen Charlotte Islands

Coast Mountains

Wet'suwet'en

Dakelh

Rocky Mountains

Plateau Region

Fraser River

Columbia Mountains

Pacific Ocean

Tsilhqot'in

Secwepemc

Stl'atl'imc

Vancouver Island

Nlaka'pamux

Okanagan Lake

Ktunaxa

N

Fraser Riv

Okanagan

Plateau Climate
• Long, cold winters
• Hot summers
• Very little precipitation in the south but more in the north

0   100   200 km

Try This

Most maps include more than one type of information. Make a list of the information on this map that can help you understand the environments of the Plateau and Interior regions. What other information does the map include?

Subarctic groups who lived along the rivers that run into the Pacific Ocean relied on salmon as well as game. This gave them much more food to dry and store for the winter.

The Plateau Region

The **Plateau** region of British Columbia is a high, flatter area of land between the Coast Mountains and the Rocky Mountains. The area to the south is quite flat, but there are more mountains as you move north. Several large rivers cross the Plateau. These carve steep cuts in the land called **canyons**.

The mix of trees in the northern Plateau is the same as in the Subarctic region, but the forests aren't as thick. The southern plateau has large areas of grass as well as desert areas where sagebrush and cacti grow.

Plateau Peoples

Aboriginal peoples in the Plateau region traditionally hunted game, fished, and gathered plants during the spring, summer, and autumn. Salmon from the rivers was a very important resource for many groups.

During the winter, Plateau peoples did a little hunting and fishing. Mostly, though, they lived off the food they had collected, dried, and stored during the rest of the year.

Plateau is the general term for any high, flat area of land. Look back at the map on page 92 to find the Plateau region of British Columbia.

White-tailed deer live in the forests of the Plateau region. When alarmed, the deer lifts its tail, flashing a white underside. This alerts the other deer in the herd to possible danger.

How To... Use First Ideas

When you have a question to answer, it's often a good idea to start by writing down your **first ideas** about what the answer might be. First ideas will get your investigation off to a good start. Here's how to use them.

1. Don't guess.
2. Think about what you already know.
3. Try to figure out the best answer.
4. As you get new information, check back to see if you should change your ideas.

Think For Yourself

Write down your first ideas about the answers to these questions:

- *In the past, do you think Subarctic peoples such as the Dunne-za [De-ney-ZA] lived in permanent villages in the winter or kept moving from place to place?*
- *Do you think Plateau peoples such as the Secwepemc [SHE-whep-m] moved from place to place in the winter?*

You might want to work with a partner. Save your ideas to check after you've finished this chapter.

Buckskin and Birch Bark

Tanned hides, snowshoes, and canoes and containers made from tree bark are traditional technologies for most Aboriginal groups in Canada. Only the peoples of the Coast and the Inuit didn't use these technologies.

Tanned Hides

Tanned hides are animal skins that are treated so that they are soft to handle or wear and they don't rot. Aboriginal groups across Canada used hides to make clothing, tents, and bags.

Almost any animal hide can be tanned. Tanned hides made from deer are called **buckskin**.

Moose, caribou, and deer were the most common skins used for clothing. To make clothing, shapes were cut out of the hide using a sharp bone or stone knife. An awl was used to punch holes along the edges. Then sinew was used to sew the pieces together.

Furs are made by leaving the animal hair on the hide. Fur robes and trims were made from bear, beaver, marmot, fox, lynx, and squirrel. Some groups also wove together strips of finer skins such as rabbit to make very soft robes.

Interior people created artwork on objects they could take with them when they moved.

Babiche (ba-BEESH) is made of thin strips of dried (but not tanned) leather. It was used as thread or woven to make bags or nets.

The basic pieces of clothing were a **tunic**, **leggings**, and **moccasins**. The style of each piece of clothing varied from group to group. Decorations included fringes, patterns made with porcupine quills, and coloured leather.

A Closer Look

Tanning Hides

Here are the basic steps for tanning a hide.

1. All of the flesh and fat is scraped off the hide while it is still warm from the animal. (At this point the hide can be kept and tanned later.)

2. The hide is washed several times, then stretched and pulled to help make it soft. Then the hide is dried, sometimes on a frame.

3. Now the hide is rubbed with animal brains and left for a day or so. (Mashed brains make the hide turn soft. Some groups add other ingredients such as eulachon oil or liver.)

4. The hide is washed again and the water is wrung out. Then the hide is attached to a frame and rubbed with a stone until it is dry and soft. This takes several hours.

5. The tanned hide is hung on a "teepee" made of sticks over a smoky fire. The smoke from the fire helps keep the hide soft. It also stops bugs and worms from chewing on it when it is stored.

Getting Around

In winter or summer, the main form of transportation for Interior peoples was walking. Many paths were made through the woods as people travelled the same routes for trading, hunting, and gathering each year. People also followed the paths made by animals.

Most of the year, people wore moccasins. In winter, when the snow was deep, they wore **snowshoes**. Snowshoes make a platform for your feet so you don't sink too deeply into the snow. This makes it easier to walk. A hunter running in snowshoes can go faster than a large animal pushing through the snow.

Canoes and Containers

Bark was a valuable resource for Interior peoples. They used it to make canoes and containers, and sometimes as covers for their shelters.

People used rivers for fishing and travelling. Many rivers have **rapids**. These are places where the water flows swiftly over rocks. Canoes made out of bark are light enough to carry around the rapids.

There were different ways to make canoes. One way was to bend the bark around a light wood frame and then sew it into place with spruce roots. Spruce gum mixed with fat made the seams waterproof.

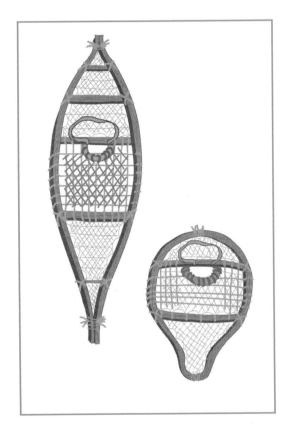

Snowshoe frames were made out of thin pieces of strong wood bent into shape and tied in place. The centres were often woven out of babiche. How do you think you would walk in snowshoes?

Birch bark makes the best canoes because it is light and bends easily. Large birch trees don't grow in every part of the Interior, though, so spruce and pine were often used instead. The strongest canoes were made from one large piece of bark. The bark was turned inside out, so the smooth part touched the water.

Some groups also made simple **dugout canoes** for travelling on lakes. A dugout canoe was carved from a single log.

Bark was also used to make a variety of containers. Food was cooked by filling a bark container with water, then placing hot rocks in the water to heat it. Other containers were made from woven spruce roots.

Find Out

Find out if anyone in your community works with hides or bark in traditional ways. Invite this person to give a demonstration to your class.

Try This

Make a display that shows a model of a bark canoe or container, buckskin clothing, or snowshoes. Include information on how the item was traditionally made. You could do this either in writing or in an oral presentation.

When you plan your project, decide what materials you'll use and how to make your display attractive.

Hunters and Dreamers

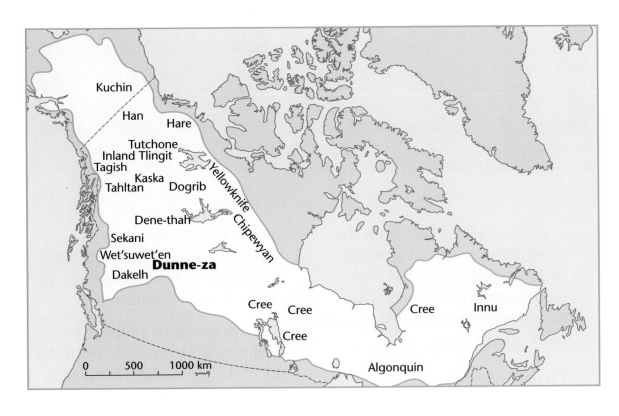

Kuchin

Han
Hare

Tutchone
Inland Tlingit
Tagish
Kaska
Tahltan   Dogrib
Yellowknife
Chipewyan

Dene-thah
Sekani
Wet'suwet'en
Dunne-za
Dakelh

Cree
Cree   Cree   Innu
Cree

0   500   1000 km

Algonquin

The Subarctic region of BC is part of a larger region that stretches across Canada. Aboriginal peoples throughout this region have similar traditions.

In this section, you can learn about the traditional culture of the Dunne-za. You can also discover how to tell moose tracks from grizzly bear tracks!

Dunne-za Communities

In the past, the Dunne-za lived in small groups made up of a few families. The groups kept moving during the year to hunt game. When there was lots of game, several families camped together. When there was less to eat, the groups split up and moved to places where they thought the hunting might be better.

A group often travelled for many days. Then, when they found a good hunting place, they stayed there for a week or so. Families travelled in one general area and returned to favourite places each year, but they didn't have permanent villages.

In summer, the Dunne-za gathered together in large groups along the Peace River. They sang, danced, and played games.

When families travelled, the men went ahead to hunt. They left signs along the trail for their families. For example, a robe on the trail meant "stop and camp." The hunter then returned to that spot, hopefully with game.

One Dreamer the Dunne-za honour is Makenunatane [mah-ke-noo-nuh-TAH-ney]. He lived during the late 1700s. He saw the arrival of Europeans in a dream and helped his people get along with the newcomers. He also encouraged peace among his own people.

Shelters were made from the materials that were available at each campsite. Branches were used to make the frames. The frames were then covered in bark, hides, or branches.

Government

The Dunne-za did not have chiefs. Each family was free to go wherever it wanted. However, the opinions of Elders and good hunters were valued.

Beliefs

In the Dunne-za tradition, Saya was the first man to follow the trails of animals. He met up with giant beasts and changed them into the ones we see today.

The Dunne-za believed that only a hunter who showed the proper respect would be successful. One sign of respect was to kill only when the group needed food or clothing.

Boys and girls spent time alone when they were around 11 or 12 years old. This was a time when they hoped to meet an animal spirit who would help them in emergencies for the rest of their lives. People did not discuss their spirit helpers with others.

Often, a spirit helper came to a person in a dream. The Dunne-za believed that dreams were powerful connections to the spirit world. Some hunters had the ability to dream of the trails where they would find game. Great Dreamers were highly respected.

Hunting Skills

To be successful, hunters had to know the ways of the animals they hunted. They needed to know the environment the animals lived in and what they ate. They also needed to know the trails they followed and what their tracks looked like.

Good hunters also knew when animals had their babies. They also watched for signs that there were fewer animals in an area than before. This told them to move to a new hunting spot while there were still some animals left to breed.

Following the Game

Throughout the year, the Dunne-za followed large forest animals such as moose and woodland caribou. These herds of animals travelled over large areas to graze on grass, bark, and leaves. They didn't always follow the same routes every year.

In some years, the herds were quite small. This made it difficult to survive in winter. People often starved to death in years when there wasn't much game.

This picture shows many Interior region animals. Which ones can you name?

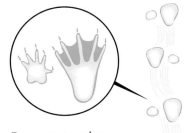

Beaver tracks

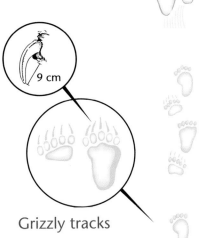

Grizzly tracks

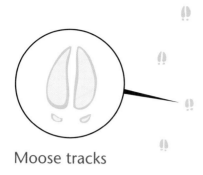

Moose tracks

Moose was the most common large game in the region. Moose are members of the deer family. They travel alone, not in large groups.

Fences to trap game were used by the peoples of the Arctic, Subarctic, Plateau, and Plains.

Snares and traps like these ones were used by all Aboriginal groups in Canada.

While they tracked large animals, the Dunne-za made sure that they travelled through areas that offered smaller game, too, such as rabbits, beavers, and grouse. These smaller animals supplied food between larger kills.

Fishing was not considered a suitable thing for Dunne-za hunters. Traditionally, the Dunne-za fished only if no other food was available.

Methods of Hunting

Snares and **traps** were used to catch both large and small game.

The snares and traps were set out where there were signs of animals. For example, a row of snares made of thick babiche might be strung across a moose trail.

Sometimes bait was used with a trap or snare to attract the animals. To remove the smell of humans, the snares and traps were rubbed with pine needles.

Moose and caribou were also hunted with bows and arrows or spears. One method was to wait in a canoe in a river. As the animals crossed the river, they weren't able to move too quickly, so they were easier targets.

Sometimes people worked together to build a V-shaped fence to trap caribou or deer travelling in large herds. As the

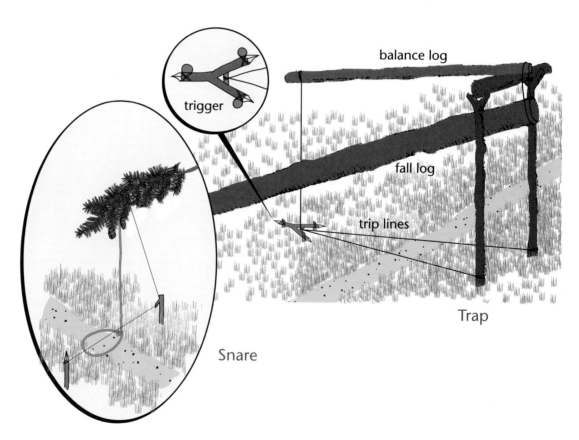

trigger

Snare

balance log

fall log

trip lines

Trap

fence narrowed, there was no place for the animals to go but towards the hunters.

Inside the fence, snares were sometimes used to trap the animals. Hunters also used spears or bows and arrows. Fences were also used to hunt buffalo herds on the flat land around the Peace River.

Sharing the Game

If a hunter returned to camp with meat, all families shared in the food.

No part of an animal was wasted. The meat, fat, bone marrow, and internal organs were eaten. The hides were tanned to make clothing, containers, and covers for shelter. Sinews of large animals were used for thread. Antlers and bones were carved into tools such as knives and bark scrapers.

Fresh meat was usually grilled on a stick over a fire. If there was extra meat, the women made **pemmican**. This is dried meat mixed with melted fat to form a paste. Sometimes berries were added to the mix. A small amount of pemmican is rich in food energy and is easy to carry while travelling.

The Dunne-za gathered some berries and plants, but these weren't as important to them as game.

Pemmican or something similar made with dried salmon was an important food for most Aboriginal groups in Canada.

Groups sometimes cached (stored) extra meat in a tree. They removed the bark so animals such as wolverines could not climb the tree and steal their meat!

Today, many Aboriginal peoples still hunt animals in their traditional territories. They eat the meat and sell the furs. It helps them meet their basic needs. Hunting also helps keep the traditions of their cultures strong.

Try This

In a group, discuss the ways hunting is important in traditional Dunne-za culture. You might want to use a **doughnut chart** to present your ideas.

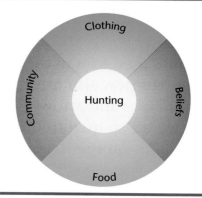

Clothing

Beliefs

Hunting

Community

Food

HOW TO... Focus Your Research

When you start to research a topic, make sure you know what information you are looking for.

1. Write down your BIG QUESTION.

2. Write down your SMALL QUESTIONS.

3. Write down what you already know or any first ideas you have.

4. Read what you've written and circle key words that might help you find information.

Find Out

Habitat is the natural home of an animal, bird, or plant.

Research one animal or bird that lives in the Interior of British Columbia, either in the Subarctic or the Plateau region. Use the facts you find to create a booklet that describes the animal or bird's **habitat** and seasonal cycle. Include information that you think would be useful to Aboriginal people living in the area.

Animals to consider: moose, elk, woodland caribou, beaver, black bear, grizzly bear, white-tailed deer, mule deer, coyote, fox, wolf, lynx, marmot, squirrel, snowshoe hare, porcupine, mountain goat, mountain sheep, grouse, eagle, raven, wood duck, Canada goose, rattlesnake, turtle.

Coyote's People

The traditional territories of the Secwepemc cover a large part of the Plateau region. In this section, you can learn how the Secwepemc lived in the past. You can also find out why they took nuts from squirrels!

Secwepemc Communities

From early spring to late autumn, most Secwepemc formed small family groups and travelled across the land to hunt, fish, and gather plants.

At their campsites, the Secwepemc built small shelters out of mats woven from **tule** (a kind of grass) or **bulrushes** (a tall water plant) placed over a frame of branches. Two families sometimes shared one shelter.

A village was made up of several homes called **pit houses**. Pit houses were made of logs and earth. They were round and were built partly underground. A pit house was always big enough for one or two families. Sometimes larger houses had 30 or 40 people living in them.

Coyote had a lot of adventures. Some of them were funny, but others were dangerous! He often tricked others to get what he wanted. Coyote stories are still told in Secwepemc communities today.

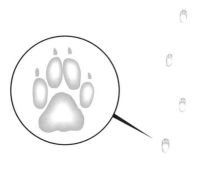

Coyote tracks

In winter, the Secwepemc gathered together to live in villages in the shelter of river valleys. Some groups returned to the same villages each winter. Other groups gathered in new places in some winters and at other times returned to their old villages.

Government

A Secwepemc village chief **inherited** his position by being the son of a chief. A chief's main job was to make sure his group met its basic needs. For example, in winter he might let others know that one family was short of food. In summer, he would decide when it was time to move to each gathering site.

Chiefs did not have special privileges. They could even lose their positions if they didn't do a good job. Elders, shamans, chiefs, and the best hunters always made the important decisions.

Beliefs

Secwepemc Elders tell many stories of the **Creation Time**. This was a time long ago when the animal spirit Coyote [Coi-O-tee] helped the Old One create the world and everything in it.

Boys and girls spent time on their own when they were around 11 or 12 years old. During this time they hoped to meet an animal spirit who would help them in emergencies during their lives. People learned special songs from their spirit helpers that they sang during winter ceremonies.

When they were alone and seeking their spirit helpers, some young people created paintings on rocks. Nobody knows what these paintings mean, but they can be found on rocks throughout the Interior of BC.

What do you think this painting means? What would it be like to be alone in the woods for many days and nights? How do you think this was good training for Aboriginal children?

The Secwepemc Seasonal Cycle

As you read this description of the seasonal cycle, imagine that you are a Secwepemc boy or girl. What would you be doing at each time of the year?

Winter

As the weather turns cold in October or November, people gather at their winter villages. The food collected over the summer is stored in cache pits. Each pit is about 1 metre deep and covered in bark. People also work together to repair old houses and build new ones.

All through the winter, men and older boys hunt deer or elk in nearby hills. They hunt alone or in a group and use dogs to track down the game. Women and children set snares near the village for rabbits and other small game. People sometimes fish through the ice in rivers.

Women and girls spend the day making clothing, baskets, and bags. People keep warm in their houses, but sit outside whenever possible—the air in a pithouse gets very smoky.

Winter is also a time for storytelling, playing games, dancing, and singing the songs of guardian spirits. When there is fresh game, people hold feasts and invite others to visit. A good feast can last three or four days!

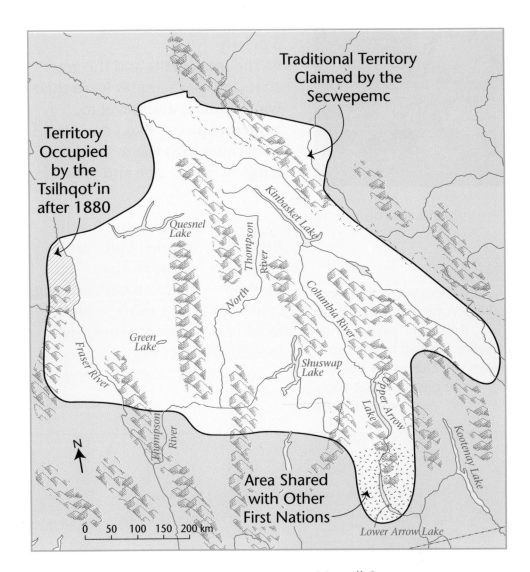

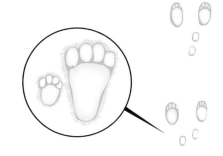

Snowshoe hare tracks

Not all Secwepemc groups followed exactly the same seasonal cycle. For example, those who had good fishing sites on the southern part of the Fraser River depended more on salmon, so they didn't travel as much to gather other food.

Saskatoon Berry

Deer were the most important large game for the Secwepemc. They were hunted in the same ways the Dunne-za hunted large game. What ways were these?

Spring

As the snow melts and the grass starts to grow, families leave their winter homes and travel to gathering places. Everyone carries something with them. They are happy to be outside and seeing new places.

Women and girls dig for the first bulbs. Steamed bulbs are a great treat for the family to eat. They also strip birch bark and dig spruce and cedar roots to use for making baskets. Men and boys look for a spruce or pine tree to make a canoe.

Soon there are fish in the streams. Small animals and birds are everywhere, and deer begin to move up into the mountains. There is plenty of game for everyone.

Summer

As spring turns to summer, Saskatoon berries begin to ripen. These are the most important berries for the Secwepemc. The first day they are ripe, women pick enough for everyone to enjoy. They hold a First Fruits ceremony to honour the berries.

As the weeks pass, there is more game to hunt and more plants to gather. Wild onions, carrots, strawberries, and gooseberries are just some of the plants that people harvest.

In early summer, different groups gather at Green Lake for trading, feasting, playing games, and arranging marriages. The Secwepemc trade goods such as dried salmon, salmon oil, deerskins, marmot robes, baskets, and hazelnuts. In return, they hope to get things they don't have in their territories, such as goat hair robes, buffalo robes, and **dentalium** [den-TAIL-eeum] **shells**.

Bulbs and roots were the most important plant food for the Secwepemc. They were dried or roasted and kept for winter. Each family had a cache pit filled with many kinds of bulbs by the end of summer.

Dentalium shells were found only in certain spots along the coast. People used the shells to make jewelry and decorate clothing. They were highly valued by all Aboriginal groups and were used as a type of money.

Lahel [lay-HEL] is a traditional game that is still popular with many Aboriginal groups in BC. The opposing team tries to guess who is holding the bone. Drummers try to confuse everyone with noise. This is one game that the Secwepemc played at their gatherings.

Chocolate Lily

Kinnickinnick

Later in summer, people go to the rivers to catch salmon as they swim upriver to lay their eggs. The men and boys fish while the women and girls dry the catch. Everyone knows that surviving the winter depends on storing as much salmon as possible.

The berries that grow near the fishing grounds are collected and dried. Women mash together some of the berries and then dry the mash to make a kind of berry cake. These cakes are eaten as treats in the winter or are used to flavour other dishes, such as soup.

Autumn

As the days grow cooler, some groups continue to fish for salmon. Others hunt deer and elk. Deer are coming down from the mountains now, so they can be easily trapped in fences built across the mountain trails. Men, women, boys, and girls all take part in the hunt.

The last of the plant foods, such as cranberries, kinnickinnick, chocolate lilies, and thistle roots, are gathered. Women and girls search for nuts hidden by the squirrels. These are especially handy because they are already shelled!

By the end of November, people collect food and hides from caches they have left on their travels. Then they head to their winter homes, and the cycle begins again.

Today, the Secwepemc live in many communities and work at many different jobs. Many Secwepemc are working to keep their culture strong and share it with others. This group is meeting in a pit house made in the traditional way.

Find Out

Do some research to find out more about one of the Interior cultures. You might want to find out about the traditional culture of one of the groups that you didn't study in this unit. Or you might want to find out about life for Aboriginal peoples today. Don't forget to focus your research before you start.

This is a Ktunaxa community around 1900. The Ktunaxa traditional territories are in the Plateau region. Many of their traditions, though, such as living in teepees and hunting buffalo, are similar to the peoples of the Plains.

Try This

One way to learn about cultures is to **compare** one to another. When you compare things, you look for the ways they are the same and the ways they are different. It helps if you write down the main ideas. This is so that you can make sure you record the same information about the things you want to compare.

Here's a chart you could use to compare how the Dunne-za and the Secwepemc met their basic needs in the past. The main ideas go in the middle boxes.

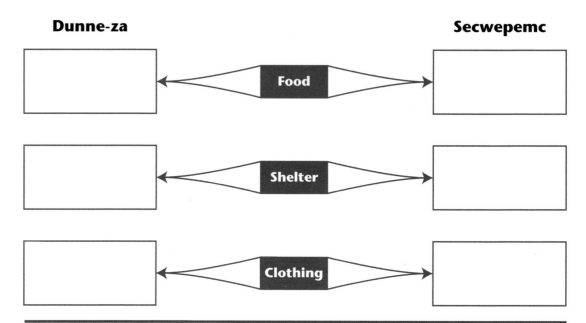

Looking Back

In this chapter, you've had a chance to learn about the traditional Aboriginal cultures of the Interior of British Columbia.

Look back at the ideas you had about the Dunne-za and Secwepemc communities at the beginning of this chapter—your first ideas. How did you do? How do you think writing down your first ideas can help you organize your investigations in social studies?

Chapter 7

Sailing into Adventure!

Adventures are exciting. They give us challenges to meet and chances to learn new things.

One type of adventure people have had through the ages is exploring. When you explore, you go someplace you've never been before. You might have explored another place when you've been on vacation. To the people who live there, walking down the street isn't an adventure. But if you don't know anything about the place, there's something new around every corner!

Just before the year 1500, Europeans began to explore North America. Unlike Aboriginal peoples, they didn't know anything about this place. So for the Europeans, it was a great adventure. In this chapter, you can find out why they came.

Back in Time

In Newfoundland, there is evidence that sailors from northern Europe, known as the **Vikings**, had reached North America in the year 985. By the 1400s, though, no one in Europe remembered this.

Aboriginal lands became part of Canada. Later on, you'll see that this created problems for Aboriginal peoples. What do you think these problems were?

The **explorers** were people from Europe. We call them explorers because they were travelling in places they had never visited before. Most of the explorers came from the countries of France, England, and Spain.

When the explorers arrived, Aboriginal peoples guided them through their traditional territories. When they returned home, the explorers reported that North America was a land with many valuable resources. They made maps of their journeys so others could follow.

Creating Canada

In time, many Europeans came to North America. They didn't come to explore, though. They came to settle here. They set up communities all across the land.

These early communities were called **colonies**. The colonies belonged to countries in Europe. After awhile, though, the settlers created their own government—the country we call Canada.

This **timeline** shows four important events in the history of Canada. Notice that there is a marker for every 50 years. A **century** is 100 years. The first century is 1400 to 1500. What is the next century?

Creating Canada

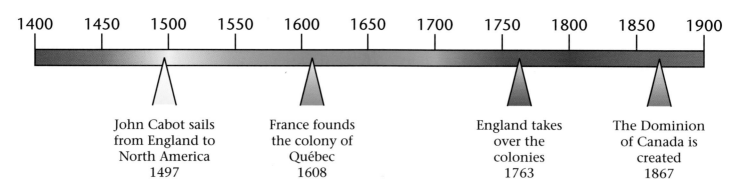

1400 1450 1500 1550 1600 1650 1700 1750 1800 1850 1900

John Cabot sails from England to North America 1497

France founds the colony of Québec 1608

England takes over the colonies 1763

The Dominion of Canada is created 1867

HOW TO...
Make a Timeline

A timeline gives a picture of time passing. The markers on a timeline are like the scale on a map. The same distance on the timeline always shows the same amount of time. Here's how to make a timeline.

1. Decide what events you want to show on the timeline. You might start by making a list.

2. Use a ruler to make a scale that you think might work. Here's an example:

Events This Week

Saturday   Sunday   Monday   Tuesday   Wednesday   Thursday   Friday

The scale for this timeline is: 1 day = 2 centimetres.

3. Try fitting your information onto the timeline. If it doesn't work, change the scale to make more time or less time pass between the markers.

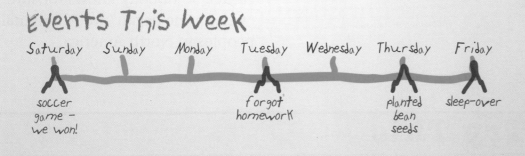

Events This Week

Saturday   Sunday   Monday   Tuesday   Wednesday   Thursday   Friday

soccer game – we won!   forgot homework   planted bean seeds   sleep-over

Think For Yourself

Make a timeline that shows three to five important events in your life so far. You could describe these events in words or show them in pictures.

European Time

The explorers recorded the dates of events according to the European system. In this system, every year is made up of 12 months, and the years are numbered in order. This is the system we still use today.

You may have heard Elders tell stories about the first people and the creation of the world.

The Time Before the Europeans

In the past, Aboriginal peoples did not keep track of time in numbered years. Aboriginal stories talk about things that happened "in the time of my great-great-grandfather" or "at the time of the floods."

This means that there are no exact dates for when Aboriginal peoples first lived in North America. Most Aboriginal cultures have stories that explain that their people have been here since the beginning of time.

Archaeologists have found evidence that Aboriginal peoples have lived here for at least 10 000 years. That's 100 centuries. This is only an approximate date, though. Other people believe there is evidence that the date could be 20 000 or 30 000 years earlier. So nobody knows for sure "when time began" for Aboriginal peoples in North America.

Try This

The Creating Canada timeline shows five centuries. Using this scale, the timeline to show 100 centuries of Aboriginal history before the arrival of Europeans would have to be 20 times longer.

Use a piece of string to show this amount of time. First, measure out the length of the Creating Canada timeline on the string. Then have a friend hold the end of the string while you measure out the length 20 times.

Now figure out how much space your own life would take up on this timeline.

Curious Columbus

The first explorers didn't know exactly where they were going or how long it would take to get there. They only knew it would be a long, dangerous voyage by sea.

In this section, you can start investigating this BIG QUESTION: *Why did the explorers do it?*

The Indies

The first explorers were looking for an ocean route to a place they called *The Indies*. This is the area that today includes the countries of China, Japan, and India on the continent of Asia.

Europeans had been trading with The Indies since the 1300s. The two goods they wanted most were silk cloth and spices such as cloves and cinnamon.

The routes from Asia to Europe were controlled by traders who charged high prices for bringing goods to Europe. The Europeans hoped to find other routes so they could get the silks and spices themselves. Anyone who found such a route was sure to become rich and famous.

Only wealthy Europeans, like these women being served dinner in 15th century France, could afford silk clothing and foods made with spices. What are some of the goods we get from other parts of the world today?

A master mariner is a person who knows enough about sailing and **navigation** to be in charge of a ship.

An explorer needed someone to pay the cost of the trip. This was usually a king or queen, or a group of traders. The explorer and the people who paid for his trip shared the profits.

To find out what *navigation*, a *log*, the *North Star*, and a *quadrant* are, read "A Closer Look: Navigation" on page 120.

Christopher Columbus

In 1492, the king and queen of Spain were interested in the ideas of a **master mariner** named Christopher Columbus. Columbus had studied every map he could find. He believed it was possible to sail from Europe to Asia across the Atlantic Ocean. The king and queen agreed to pay for a voyage to find out.

To the Edge of the World

Christopher Columbus and his three ships, the *Santa Maria*, the *Niña*, and the *Pinta*, left Spain on 3 August 1492. We know quite a bit about the trip from Columbus's point of view because a copy of his **log** has survived to this day.

The ships sailed for two months, with no land in sight. In those days, many people believed that the earth was flat. The crew became afraid that if they kept sailing in one direction, they might fall off the edge of the world. So they threatened to **mutiny**—they were going to take over the ship!

Columbus found out that his crew planned to push him overboard. Then they were going to tell everyone back home that he had fallen into the ocean when he stood too close to the railing to take a reading of the **North Star** with his **quadrant**.

Luckily, Columbus was able to convince his crew to give him more time. Finally, on October 12th, they sighted land.

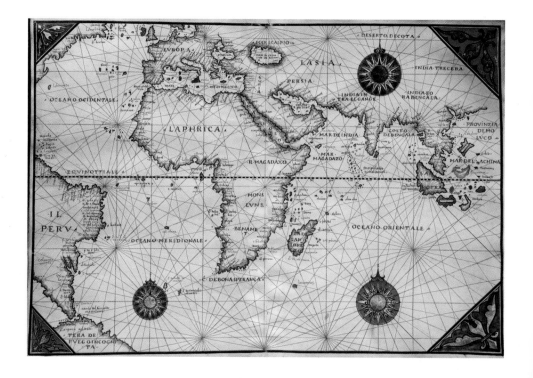

This is what Columbus and most people of the time thought the world was like. Can you see the shapes of Europe on the left and Asia on the right? Which continents are missing? Which are the wrong shapes?

Columbus Makes a Mistake

Columbus explored the new lands he had reached, then he returned to Spain early in 1493. He reported that he had reached an unknown part of The Indies.

But Columbus was wrong. He had actually reached the islands we now call the Caribbean. (See the map on page 122.) Columbus called the people he met on the islands Indians. This name was used to describe Aboriginal peoples of North America for many years. Today, Aboriginal peoples prefer to be called by the names of their groups, such as Dunne-za or Haida.

This is how the *Santa Maria* and the *Niña* might have looked at sea. What information do you think an artist would use to create a picture of something that happened long ago?

Think For Yourself

Imagine you are Christopher Columbus. Your crew wants you to end your journey and return to Spain. What reasons would you give to convince them to carry on?

Now imagine you are a member of the crew. What reasons would you give to convince Columbus to turn back?

You might want to act out this scene in a group. The picture on page 128 shows how people dressed at the time, if you'd like to make costumes.

After his first trip, Columbus crossed the Atlantic three more times. When he died in 1506, he still believed he had reached Asia.

Navigation

Navigation is the act of directing the course of a ship from one place to another. In the 1500s, there were only simple tools to help sailors navigate. It wasn't easy to be accurate.

Sailors kept on course by keeping track of the direction they were travelling and the distance travelled. The captain of the ship kept a log to record these readings and other events on the ship each day.

Log
North: 10 kilometres
West: 5 kilometres
Southwest: 10 kilometres

FINISH   START

Direction

By looking at a **compass** while facing the same direction as the **bow** (front) of the ship, a sailor could tell the direction in which the ship was sailing.

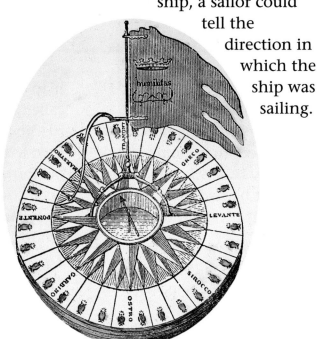

The needle in a compass is made of a metal that is attracted like a magnet to the North Pole. The needle always points to the north, so from this you can figure out south, east, and west.

Speed and Distance

If he knew the speed the ship had been travelling and how long it had been travelling at that speed, a sailor could figure out the distance travelled.

Speed: 5 kilometres per hour
Time at that speed: 2 hours
Distance travelled: 2 x 5 = 10 kilometres

In the days of Columbus, sailors probably estimated their speed based on experience. Later, in the 1500s, sailors used a **log line** to get a closer estimate.

Sandglasses were used to keep time. It took half an hour for the sand to flow from one part of the glass to the other. Then the glass was turned over.

Location

A **quadrant** was an instrument sailors used to figure out how far north or south of the Equator they were.

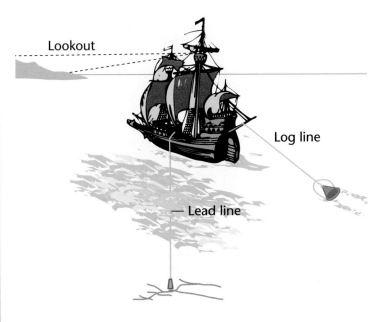

Lookout

Log line

— Lead line

Sailors dropped the end of a log line into the water. The faster the ship was going, the faster the rope unreeled. Knots were placed at even spaces along the line. Sailors then counted the knots to figure out the speed. The lead line was used to tell how deep the water was.

As you go further from the Equator, the sun appears to be lower in the sky. Looking at the sun with a quadrant told a sailor how low the sun was. This reading was compared to a reference book to find out the ship's location. In the Northern Hemisphere, sailors used the North Star to take readings at night.

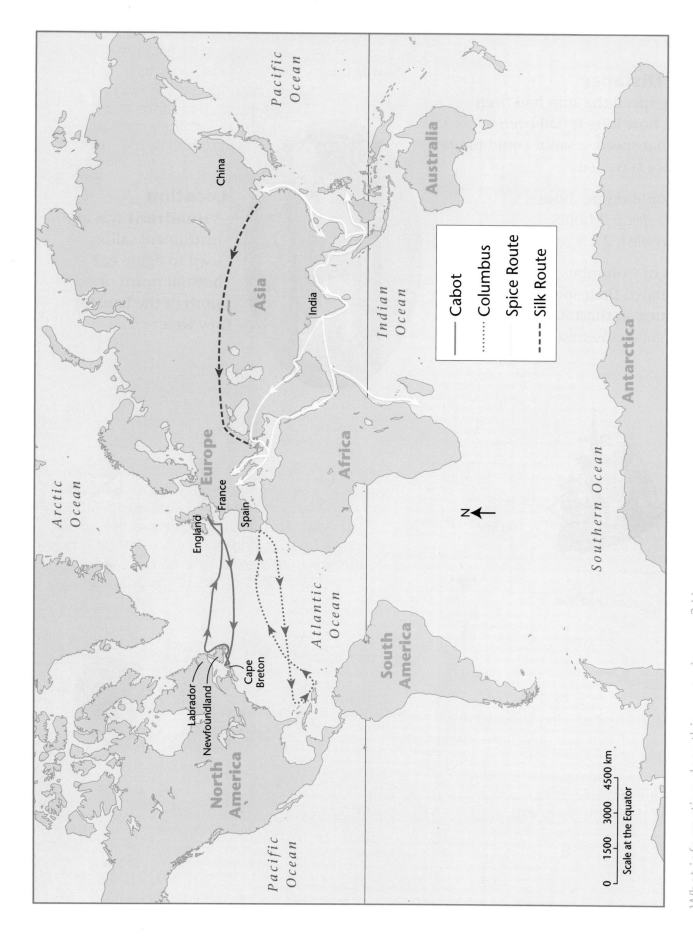

China

Pacific
Ocean

Australia

Asia

India

Indian
Ocean

Cabot
Columbus
Spice Route
Silk Route

Europe

Africa

Antarctica

N

France

Spain

England

Southern Ocean

Arctic
Ocean

Labrador

Newfoundland

Cape
Breton

Atlantic
Ocean

South
America

North
America

Pacific
Ocean

0   1500   3000   4500 km

Scale at the Equator

What information does this map give you? Use your finger to trace the routes. What do you think it means when one route has arrows going in two directions?

Cabot Sets Sail

Everyone in Europe was excited by Columbus's news that he had reached an unknown part of Asia—they still didn't know about North America. Now European countries had another reason to explore. Each wanted to be the first to find more new lands.

When a country takes over another land, the new land becomes a colony. European countries hoped to set up colonies that were rich in resources that could be sent back to Europe.

The English Join In

In 1497, King Henry VII of England gave the explorer John Cabot permission to claim lands for England. Henry VII was interested in Cabot's idea that he could reach Asia by sailing across the northern part of the Atlantic Ocean.

The **merchants** of an English town called Bristol paid for Cabot's trip. Merchants are people whose main job is trading. They hoped to make a lot of money if Cabot found a new route to The Indies.

From the Europeans' point of view, North America was a "new" land waiting to be "discovered." What do you think Aboriginal people's point of view was?

Check the map on page 122 to compare Columbus's and Cabot's routes.

We don't know what Cabot or his ship looked like. This painting of Cabot setting sail from Bristol was painted by a Canadian artist, Harold Goodridge, in 1947. What can you tell about European culture from this painting?

Henry VII

King Henry VII of England gave John Cabot permission to:

> *seeke out, discover, and finde whatsoever isles, countries, regions or provinces of the heathens and infidels*

Do you understand what Henry VII said? If you don't, it's because the English language has changed since 1497. One job of the historian is to read old documents like this and figure out what they mean. In today's English, Henry VII was saying something like "Find lands where heathens and infidels live."

This document tells us something about the English king's point of view. **Heathens and infidels** are people who do not follow the Christian belief system. Henry VII believed that people who were not Christians did not have **rights** to their lands. Rights are things that are fair for people to have or do.

Most Europeans of the time thought that taking over these lands and persuading the people to become Christians was a good thing. They believed they were helping the people. So persuading people to become Christians was another reason for exploring.

Watch out for spies! The best source of information on Cabot's voyage is a letter written to Columbus. Historians think the letter was from a Spanish spy at the English court who heard Cabot's report to the king.

Crossing the Atlantic

Cabot set sail from Bristol in a ship called the *Matthew* near the end of May 1497. He used his compass and quadrant to try to keep sailing straight west. He didn't really know if this would work, though.

Cabot was travelling further north than Columbus had. The weather was cold. There was the danger of hitting an iceberg. As the days passed, Cabot's crew became worried and frightened. Cabot tried to keep everyone calm. He encouraged them to keep going.

On 24 June 1497, they saw signs that they were nearing land—seagulls and other birds flying overhead and bits of plants and trees floating in the water. Soon the lookout shouted that land was in sight!

We don't know exactly where the *Matthew* landed. It might have been at what we now call Newfoundland, Labrador, or Cape Breton. (See the map on page 122.) Cabot believed he had reached another unknown part of The Indies.

When they landed, they saw snares and signs of a campfire. They didn't see any people, though. Cabot put up flags and a cross (an important symbol to Christians), and claimed the land for the king of England.

Buckets of Fish

Cabot sailed along the coast hoping to find people to trade with. Instead, he found shores lined with forests and oceans filled with cod fish. There were so many fish that the sailors could catch them just by dipping buckets into the water alongside the ship.

Eventually Cabot gave up finding people to trade with. He set sail back to England and arrived in Bristol on 6 August 1497. There, he told everyone that he had claimed a part of The Indies for England. He also told amazing tales about all the fish they had found!

In 1997, this copy of the *Matthew* sailed from Bristol to Newfoundland to celebrate the 500th anniversary of Cabot's voyage. What could people learn from following an explorer's journey?

REAL PEOPLE: JOHN CABOT (?–C. 1498)

John Cabot was a master mariner and a trader from Italy. His family made its money trading for spices and other goods from The Indies. Cabot was highly respected for his skill in using a quadrant and a similar instrument called an **astrolabe**. All his life it had been his dream to find a new route to The Indies.

We're not sure how old Cabot was when he travelled to North America. We do know that he had a wife named Mattea and that they had at least three sons.

A Mystery at Sea

Even though Cabot didn't come back with any trade goods, the English were pleased with his news. In 1498, he left England to sail the Atlantic again. This time he had five ships. We don't know what happened, but none of the ships was ever seen again.

Cabot had reached the Eastern Woodlands region. The land here is gently rolling, with many lakes and rivers. At the time, the area was covered in a mixed forest of trees such as oak, maple, elm, pine, hemlock, and spruce.

Do you have any ideas about what might have happened to John Cabot and his ships?

Try This

This chapter explains three reasons for the journeys of the early explorers.

Summarize these three reasons. When you summarize something, you write down the BIG IDEAS, but not all the *details*. You might need to skim this section and the section called "Curious Columbus" on pages 117 to 122 to get the information you need.

A Sailor's Life

At the time Europeans first began to explore North America, sailing ships were the main form of transportation for travelling across the oceans.

The Ships

Ships came in different shapes and sizes—just like cars do today. Over the centuries, shipbuilders kept designing better ships that could carry more goods and were easier to handle.

The captain was in charge of the ship. Most of the crew were regular sailors. Sailors often started out as **ship's boys** when they were as young as nine or ten years old.

There were also a few men who had special jobs, such as the navigator, the carpenter, and the sail-maker. One important crew member was the ship's cat—rats were a big problem on board ships!

Back in these days, women were not allowed to be sailors. The first woman we know to sail around the world was a French girl named Jean Baré. She made the trip in 1768 disguised as a ship's boy.

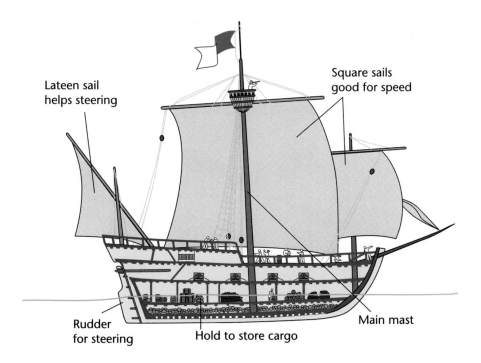

Lateen sail helps steering

Square sails good for speed

Rudder for steering

Hold to store cargo

Main mast

In the 1400s and 1500s, the **caravel** was a popular type of ship. Two of Columbus's ships, the *Pinta* and the *Niña*, and Cabot's *Matthew* were probably caravels. About 15 to 20 caravels would probably fit in one medium-sized ferry today.

You can see the crow's nest in the photograph of the *Matthew* on page 125. It is the round balcony near the top of the main mast. What do you think it would be like up there as the ship tossed and rolled through the waves?

Unless it was very cold, sailors usually worked in bare feet. Bare feet don't slip on wet decks and make it easier to climb rope ladders. What else do you notice about the way these sailors are dressed?

The Work Day

Work on a ship went on 24 hours a day. Someone had to be steering and watching the course all the time. One sailor watched in the **crow's nest** to keep a lookout for danger, such as white water, which could mean rocks.

Other sailors climbed up and down masts to tend the sails. If the wind was strong, sails had to be rolled up or the wind might push the boat over. This was dangerous work in a storm!

Sailors usually worked in **watches**—four hours working and four hours off. Ship's boys worked alongside the sailors. They helped with jobs such as scrubbing the decks, tending the sails, repairing ropes, and checking for leaks. There was always work to do.

Home at Sea

The captain had a cabin. Sailors, though, usually ate and slept on deck unless it was very cold. Below deck, it was crowded and dirty, and there wasn't any fresh air.

At the beginning of the voyage, the ship was stocked with fresh water and food that would keep, such as salted fish and meat, dried peas, and hard biscuits. Most meals were the same every day: biscuits and **pottage**, a soup or stew made of boiled fish and peas.

After many days at sea, pale, wiggly beetles called **weevils** usually got into the biscuits. Sailors had to shake the bugs out before taking a bite! The drinking water smelled, and there were usually bugs floating in it. Sometimes the sailors were given beer to drink instead.

Fun and Games

If the weather was good, sailors played games, told stories, or sang and danced. One game was to see who could climb to the top of the tallest mast the fastest.

Of course, the best times happened when the ship arrived at an exciting new place. Sailors saw the world and had adventures that **landlubbers** only dreamed of.

A landlubber is someone who doesn't have any experience at sea.

Find Out

What do you think life was like for a ship's boy? Exciting? Boring? Dangerous? Fun? Was it some or all of these things? Write down your first idea.

Use information in this section to check your idea. Find one or two more facts at the library or on the Internet. You might use these headings for taking notes: Food, Clothing, Work, Fun.

A ship's boy's life was _____

Food	Clothing
Work	Fun

Looking Back

In this chapter, you found out something about why Europeans came to North America. You also saw that different cultures have different ways of recording time.

How do you think timelines can help you understand history?

Chapter 8

Welcoming the Explorers

*C*abot had not arrived at the shores of an empty land. The coast he sailed past is the traditional territory of the Mi'kmaq. Imagine how the arrival of the Europeans might have been from the Mi'kmaq's point of view.

What would you do if you looked up and saw a strange vessel coming towards you? What would you think if you saw people whose skin was a colour you had never seen before? (Imagine bright blue!) How would you feel about this?

When explorers and Aboriginal peoples first met, they both had a lot to learn about getting along with people from other cultures. In this chapter, you can find out what happened when the Haudenosaunee met the French.

European Culture

Who were the Europeans? What were they like?

You have seen that Aboriginal cultures in North America had some similarities and some differences. European cultures also had similarities and differences. Here are some of the things European cultures had in common around 1500.

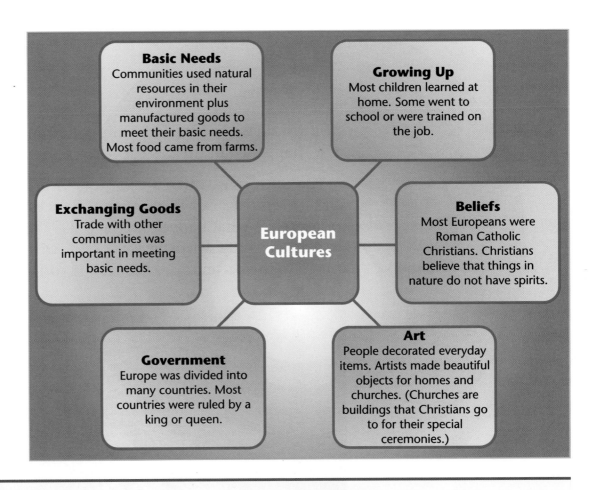

European Cultures

Basic Needs
Communities used natural resources in their environment plus manufactured goods to meet their basic needs. Most food came from farms.

Growing Up
Most children learned at home. Some went to school or were trained on the job.

Exchanging Goods
Trade with other communities was important in meeting basic needs.

Beliefs
Most Europeans were Roman Catholic Christians. Christians believe that things in nature do not have spirits.

Government
Europe was divided into many countries. Most countries were ruled by a king or queen.

Art
People decorated everyday items. Artists made beautiful objects for homes and churches. (Churches are buildings that Christians go to for their special ceremonies.)

Try This

Compare this European culture web with the culture web for Aboriginal peoples on page 50. Work with a partner. That way, you can each open your book to a different culture web.

What do you notice about the similarities and differences between these two cultures? You could use a **Venn diagram** like the one shown here to compare them. Start by putting the similarities in the middle.

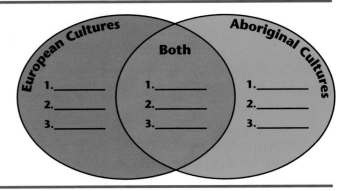

What Really Happened?

How do we know what really happened in the past?

The truth is, we often aren't sure. This is because we can't see for ourselves what happened. If we want to study seashells, we can go to the ocean to see the real thing. When we study history, though, we can't go back in time.

Evidence from the Past

To study history, we have to rely on evidence from the past. This

Some Aboriginal groups recorded events in pictures. This is a pictograph carved into rock by the Mi'kmaq. What does it show?

includes **artifacts**, such as tools and clothing that have been saved from days long ago.

Evidence also includes what people say about what happened in the past. We have evidence about the days of the explorers in the stories Aboriginal Elders tell us. We also have evidence in the historical **documents** that were written by the explorers and other Europeans at the time.

Do the Stories Match?

Sometimes different accounts of the same event don't exactly match. This might be because mistakes were made when the facts were written down. It might also be because different people saw the event from different points of view.

This can happen in any situation. There could even be three or four different **versions** of the same event. People's personal knowledge, beliefs, and feelings affect how they see things. When you read about the past, make sure you consider all points of view. Then you can use this information to form your own opinion about what happened.

Documents might include logs, diaries, newspaper articles, books, and letters.

Think For Yourself

When you hear two different versions of the same event, stop and ask questions that help you sort the facts from the opinions. Try practising with this example.

Maia and Tony play on opposite baseball teams. This is what they have to say about a game they played against each other.

Maia: *It was a great game! It rained a little, but that didn't stop us from playing our best. There were a couple of close calls, but the umpire got it right every time.*

Tony: *The game was a washout. The weather was lousy and the umpire didn't pay any attention to what was going on.*

Answer these questions yourself, then compare your answers with a partner's answers.

- *Whose team won the game?*
- *What makes you think this?*
- *What facts about the game can you tell from reading these two points of view?*

Can you think of a recent event in which you had a different point of view than someone else? Why did this happen?

First Sightings

We don't know exactly when or where Aboriginal peoples and Europeans first saw each other. The evidence makes historians think it was soon after Cabot's journey in 1497.

After Cabot's voyage, many fishers from Europe sailed to the waters around Newfoundland to catch cod. Fish were a valuable resource to the Europeans. Europe was a fairly small place. The farmers couldn't supply all the food they needed for the many people who lived there. For some Europeans, their beliefs also required them to eat fish rather than meat on many days of the year.

The fishers came ashore to fix their nets or to get food, water, and wood. They also needed to dry the fish they caught so that they wouldn't rot on the trip home. This was when Aboriginal peoples and Europeans met for the first time.

The Mi'kmaq Dream

Many Aboriginal groups say shamans knew Europeans were coming before they actually arrived. Often, the idea came to a person in a dream.

One of the first descriptions of meeting from the Aboriginal peoples' point of view is a story told by Mi'kmaq Elders. We don't know who the Europeans were.

This timeline shows the explorers you learned about in Chapter 7 and Jacques Cartier, who is described in this chapter. How many years are there between each two markers on this timeline?

Making Contact

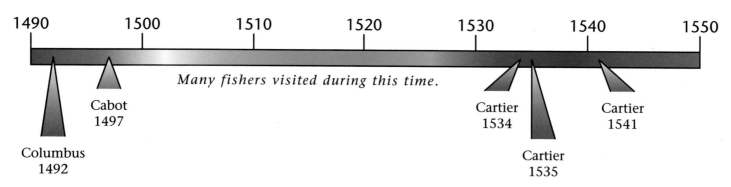

1490   1500   1510   1520   1530   1540   1550

Many fishers visited during this time.

Cabot
1497

Columbus
1492

Cartier
1534

Cartier
1535

Cartier
1541

The Mi'kmaq traditional territories are along the coast of Nova Scotia and on Prince Edward Island. In the past, the Mi'kmaq were hunters and gatherers. They built fishing camps along the shore in summer.

In The Words Of...

The Mi'kmaq Elders

In this story, a young woman dreams she sees a small island with trees floating towards the land. The next day, the people see Europeans for the first time.

When they got up in the morning, they saw what seemed to be a small island that had drifted near to the land and became fixed there. There were trees on the island, and what seemed to be a number of bears were crawling about on the branches.

All the Mi'kmaq men seized their bows and arrows and spears, and rushed down to the shore to shoot the bears. But they stopped in surprise when they saw that the creatures were not bears but men. And what seemed to be a small island with trees was really a large boat with long poles rising above it.

Excerpt used with permission from *I Have Lived Here Since the World Began* by Arthur J. Ray (Toronto: Key Porter Books Ltd and Lester Publishing, 1996).

Think For Yourself

These questions might help you think about seeing Europeans from the Mi'kmaq point of view.

- *Why might the Mi'kmaq think the ship was an island with trees?*
- *Why might the Mi'kmaq first think that the men were bears?*

You might want to write down your answers, then make a drawing to show what you think the ship looked like.

The European Point of View

In 1534, the French explorer Jacques Cartier described the people he saw in the area of Newfoundland. This is the first description we have of Aboriginal peoples from the European point of view.

In The Words Of...

Jacques Cartier

From the evidence we have, historians think Cartier could be describing the Beothuk. We know that they painted their bodies and that they lived in this area.

[Their] bodies are fairly well formed but they are wild and savage folk. They wear their hair tied up on the top of their heads like a handful of twisted hay, and into it they weave a few birds' feathers. They clothe themselves with the fur of animals, both men as well as women. They [all] paint themselves with certain tan colours. They have canoes made of birch bark...from which they catch many seals.

Think For Yourself

Cartier described the Beothuk as "wild and savage," even though he hadn't met them. In a group, discuss why you think he described them this way. In what way are his comments biased?

In Search of the Northwest Passage

European traders soon realized that Cabot had not actually reached The Indies. They now knew the continent of North America was between Europe and Asia.

They didn't give up on finding a route, though. They had another idea. They thought they might be able to cross North America by water. They called this route the **Northwest Passage**.

Jacques Cartier was one of the first explorers to search for the Northwest Passage. You read Cartier's description of the Beothuk in the last section. Now you can find out more about his voyages.

A French Explorer

Jacques Cartier made three trips to North America between 1534 and 1541. The king of France paid for his voyages. During this time, Cartier kept a journal of what happened. After, he wrote a book based on his journals. Everything we know about Cartier's adventures comes from this book.

REAL PEOPLE: JACQUES CARTIER (1497–1557)

Jacques Cartier came from the French **port** of St. Malo. A port is a town on the ocean. Many men from St. Malo made regular trips across the Atlantic Ocean to the Grand Banks to fish. Cartier probably made such trips before he first began to explore. His experience as a sailor made him a good choice when the king of France wanted an explorer.

There are no pictures of Cartier painted at the time. The picture shown here was done in 1836 for a French book about clothing styles.

The First Voyage

Cartier's first voyage took place in the summer of 1534. He travelled with two ships and 61 sailors. It took them only 20 days to cross the Atlantic.

Cartier sailed around the northern tip of Newfoundland. He arrived at a body of water he called the St. Lawrence. It was actually a **gulf** at the mouth of a large river. The water's strong current made Cartier think there must be a river nearby. He thought this might be the Northwest Passage.

Cartier spent the summer exploring the coast and looking for the river. But the Gulf of St. Lawrence was so large, he missed finding the river. During this time, he made contact with two different Aboriginal groups: the Mi'kmaq and the Haudenosaunee.

A gulf is a large bay of water. Even today, the rocky coast, strong winds, and shallow waters make the East Coast a challenge for sailors.

Contact is the word we use to describe what happens when people from two cultures meet.

This map shows Cartier's first voyage in 1534.

0 100 200 300 km

Anticosti Island

Gaspé

Chaleur Bay

Bay Cartier called St Lawrence

Newfoundland

Stadacona

N

Hochelaga

Lachine Rapids

To France

From France

○   Points at which Cartier missed the entrance to the St. Lawrence River

—— Cartier's Route

Contact with the Mi'kmaq

When the Mi'kmaq of Prince Edward Island saw Cartier, they greeted him by waving furs on the ends of sticks. They called to him to show that they were friendly and wanted to trade.

Cartier and the Mi'kmaq first exchanged a few gifts. Then they got down to trading. The Europeans offered knives, necklaces, beads, and **ironware**. Ironware are metal items such as pots. The Mi'kmaq were eager to trade. They traded away all their furs— even the ones they were wearing!

Contact with the Haudenosaunee

As Cartier continued to explore, he came across a group of Haudenosaunee [ha-duh-nuh-SAH-nee]. They had come to fish in the region we know as the Gaspé Peninsula. The Haudenosaunee were from the village of Stadacona, further up the St. Lawrence River. Their leader was called Donnacona.

The Haudenosaunee were also eager to trade their furs with Cartier. Cartier traded with them, but his real goal was to claim the land for France. He was sure he was no longer on an island. Instead, he believed he had found a continent that could provide France with many resources. Two days later he put up a large cross. Across the top he wrote *"Vive le Roi de France!"*—"Long Live the King of France!"

Donnacona was not happy about the cross. He didn't know what the writing said, but he thought the cross was a symbol that Cartier was claiming rights to the land.

In the past, the people along the upper St. Lawrence River and around the Great Lakes lived year-round in villages made up of wooden longhouses. They hunted and fished. They also had farms.

In The Words Of...

Jacques Cartier

In his journal, Cartier tells us what Donnacona did when he saw the cross he had put up. A harangue is when someone angrily tells you his or her opinion.

When we had returned to our ships, the captain [village headman], dressed in an old black bearskin, arrived in a canoe with three of his sons and his brother.... And pointing to the cross he made us a long harangue, making the sign of the cross with two of his fingers; and then he pointed to the land all around about, as if he wished to say that all this region belonged to him, and that we ought not to have set up this cross without his permission.

Cartier calmed Donnacona by lying. He used signs to suggest that the marker was there only to help him find his way.

Kidnapped!

After Cartier put up the cross, he had his men capture Donnacona and his sons. On board his ship, Cartier gave the Haudenosaunee many gifts. Then he explained that he wanted to take Donnacona's sons to France with him.

Cartier wanted to show the young men to the king of France. He also wanted them to learn French so that they could be his guides when he returned to the St. Lawrence. He made it seem like an invitation, but Cartier was really kidnapping the men.

Donnacona did not put up a fight. It might be that he didn't know what Cartier was saying—the French and Haudenosaunee spoke different languages. Or it might be that the Haudenosaunee knew they couldn't win a fight if they tried to rescue the young men. We only have Cartier's point of view, though, so we don't know for sure what happened. The next day, Cartier sailed back to France with Donnacona's sons.

What Cartier Found Out

Cartier learned these important things on his first voyage:

- He discovered that Newfoundland is an island.

- He located the continent of North America.

At the time, explorers often captured people as proof that they had been to distant lands. In their culture, this wasn't a wrong thing to do.

Try This

Even though the information we have about events is from Cartier's point of view, there is evidence that Donnacona and Cartier disagreed about who had rights to the land.

Check back to find evidence of this disagreement. Then use a chart like this one to show Donnacona's and Cartier's different points of view.

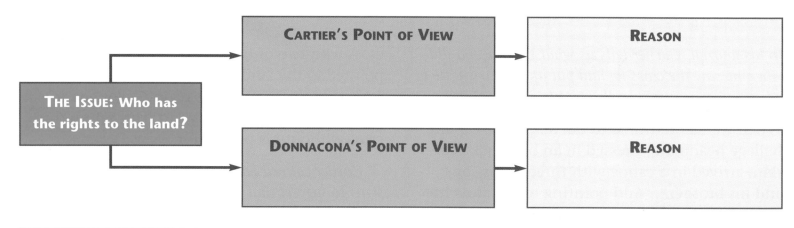

THE ISSUE: Who has the rights to the land?

CARTIER'S POINT OF VIEW → REASON

DONNACONA'S POINT OF VIEW → REASON

A Second Voyage

Cartier returned to the Gulf of St. Lawrence the next year, in 1535. Donnacona's sons were with him. They guided Cartier to the village of Stadacona. This time the French planned to spend the winter. Although Donnacona tried to make friends with Cartier, Cartier didn't trust him, so the French made their own camp.

A Misunderstanding

Cartier then decided to explore further up the St. Lawrence River in search of the Northwest Passage.

At first it seemed as though Donnacona was going to help Cartier. But then Donnacona said Cartier couldn't go up the river because it was his territory. Cartier thought Donnacona was being unfriendly and unhelpful for no reason.

Historians who have read Cartier's journals think that Cartier didn't understand Donnacona and the Haudenosaunee. Donnacona wanted one of his people to stay with the French and a French person to stay with the Haudenosaunee. In his culture, this was a sign of friendship and respect for Donnacona's rights to the river. But Cartier didn't want to do this. So Donnacona thought Cartier was being unfriendly and unhelpful.

Cartier ignored Donnacona and sailed up the river as far as the Haudenosaunee village of Hochelaga. There he ran into strong rapids. The European boats were too large and heavy to carry around the rapids. Disappointed, Cartier returned to his camp near Stadacona. He knew that this river was not the Northwest Passage.

A Miserable Winter

As winter came, Cartier and his men built a shelter. It was a miserable time. The winter was colder than any they had ever known. The snow was so deep it was up to their armpits.

In the middle of winter, Cartier's men began to get sick from **scurvy**. Men were dying every day. Cartier tried to hide

At this time, Europeans began calling the region *Canada*. This may have been because Donnacona's sons used a similar sounding word to direct Cartier to their village.

Find Stadacona and Hochelaga on the map on page 138. What Aboriginal technology could have helped Cartier with his river trips?

Scurvy is a disease that is caused by a lack of vitamin C. People with scurvy get swollen arms and legs. Their gums rot and their teeth fall out. Eventually they die. Sailors on long voyages often got scurvy.

Do you think this painting shows the Aboriginal or European point of view of this event? What are the clues?

the deaths from the Haudenosaunee. He was sure that if the Haudenosaunee knew, they would attack them.

Instead, when the Haudenosaunee found out they helped the French. They showed them how to make a tea from parts of the white cedar tree. The tea was rich in vitamin C. It cured the men who were sick and kept everyone healthy for the rest of the winter.

More Kidnappings

During the winter, Donnacona told Cartier about lands nearby that were rich in minerals. Cartier thought Donnacona was talking about gold and silver. (Historians now think he was talking about copper. Copper was valuable in Aboriginal trading.) This gave him an idea. He wanted to set up a French colony along the St. Lawrence. This would be a base from which they could search for gold.

Now Cartier had to convince the king of France that this was a good idea. Once again, he decided to take back a Haudenosaunee to tell the king about these treasures. This time he kidnapped Donnacona and nine others before he returned to France in the spring.

What Cartier Found Out

Cartier didn't find the Northwest Passage on his second voyage. He did learn these things, though:

- There was a large river and several small rivers that could be used to travel the land.

- It was possible for Europeans to survive the winter in the land known as Canada.

Try This

Check back to the chart you made showing Donnacona's and Cartier's points of view about rights to the land. Did the events on Cartier's second voyage fit with the ideas you wrote on the chart?

The First Colony

After the second voyage, Cartier arrived back in France with his captives. Donnacona told the king about the riches in his homeland. Then Cartier was able to convince the king that it was a good idea to explore this land they now called Canada.

The king decided to set up a colony there. He did not put Cartier in charge, though. Instead, he asked a man called Jean-François de la Rocque de Roberval to run the colony.

Cartier wasn't happy about this, but the king had made up his mind. Then there was more bad news. During the winter, Donnacona and all of his group except one girl died from European diseases.

The Colony Fails

In 1541, Cartier returned to Stadacona with the first French **colonists**. (He didn't bring back the Haudenosaunee girl who was still alive, though.)

How do you think Donnacona's death will affect Cartier's return to the St. Lawrence?

Colonists are people who settle in a place when a country wants to claim an area of land. Having people from the country living in the colony helps make the claim stronger.

REAL PEOPLE: DONNACONA (?–C. 1540)

All we know about Donnacona comes from what Cartier tells us. We don't have any pictures of him or know what it was like for him to "discover" Europe. We know he learned to speak a little French and was often a guest at the king's court.

Donnacona seems to have been interested in new ideas. His actions show that he was worried, though, about what would happen to his people if the Europeans started to control things.

It seems Donnacona was loved by his people. When Cartier kidnapped him, the Haudenosaunee offered their most valuable goods to Cartier in exchange for their leader.

This is a painting of the Haudenosaunee showing the French a cure for scurvy. Do you think it is in the tradition of European art or Aboriginal art? What are the clues?

Because of Cartier's mistake, the French came up with a saying: Something that is a fake is called a "Canadian diamond."

The colonists were French convicts who had been released from prison when they agreed to make the trip with Cartier. (It was hard to find people who were willing to go on such an adventure!) Roberval planned to follow later with more colonists.

When they arrived at Stadacona again, Cartier met the new Haudenosaunee leader, Agona. He told him that Donnacona was dead, but that the other Haudenosaunee were living in France as wealthy and important people. He thought Agona would be pleased to know that Donnacona would not be coming back to take over as leader.

At first everyone was friendly. Then things changed. The Haudenosaunee tried to make life hard for the French. Eventually some of the colonists were killed by the Haudenosaunee. We don't know exactly why. Historians think the Haudenosaunee might not have believed Cartier's lies about their people in France.

After ten months, Cartier and his group left. When Roberval arrived with more colonists, they didn't do any better. They left a year later.

Gold and Diamonds

Cartier returned to France with samples of what he thought were gold and diamonds. But the stones were actually iron pyrites and **quartz**—a kind of clear rock. People at the king's court laughed at Cartier's mistake. He retired from the sea and spent the rest of his life in St. Malo.

Try This

Make a timeline that shows Jacques Cartier's three voyages. Include a drawing of each voyage that shows what happened from the Haudenosaunee point of view.

Think For Yourself

When we investigate the actions of a person in the past, we often ask a BIG QUESTION such as "What was this person's contribution to Canada?" SMALL QUESTIONS can help sort the facts from the opinions.

Here are some questions to ask yourself about Jacques Cartier:

- *What successes did he have on his voyages?*
- *What troubles did he cause for himself and for others?*
- *What part of his journeys interested you the most?*

You might need to skim this chapter to collect the facts you need. You could record your notes in a chart like this one.

Successes	Troubles	Interesting

Looking Back

In this chapter, you saw that Aboriginal peoples welcomed the Europeans. You also learned that the Haudenosaunee and the French had different points of view about rights to the land.

Why is considering different points of view an important part of social studies?

Chapter 9

The Fur Trade

For about 60 years after Cartier's colony failed, France gave up the idea of settling along the St. Lawrence River. Europeans decided that the only valuable resource in the area was fish, and they didn't need to live there to catch them!

In time, the Europeans found that Aboriginal peoples had something else they wanted—furs. People in Europe were willing to pay a lot of money for furs, especially beaver fur. Soon people came to the St. Lawrence just to trade for furs.

In this chapter, you can find out how the fur trade got started and why it led to more exploration. You'll also see how the French finally started a colony along the St. Lawrence.

Fashionable Furs

Aboriginal peoples set up the first **fur-trading posts**. A trading post is a place where traders meet to exchange goods.

Tadoussac [TA-doo-sak], a place on the St. Lawrence River, was one of the early trading posts. Tadoussac had always been a place where Aboriginal groups met to trade in the summer. You can locate Tadoussac on the map on page 151.

Most of the trading was between Aboriginal peoples of the Subarctic region and peoples from the Great Lakes area. The Subarctic peoples had top-quality furs to trade. This is because the winters are colder in the north, so the animals grow thicker furs. People from the Great Lakes area had corn to trade. Ground corn is a good food for travelling, but it is too cold in the north to grow corn.

European traders fit into this system by coming to Tadoussac to do their own trading. By the early 1600s, about 1000 ships a year came from Europe to trade in the spring and summer.

For trade to work, each side must have something the other side wants.

Europeans had never seen corn before coming to North America.

This painting shows a trading post at Montreal. What details did the artist include to make the painting interesting?

Luxury items are things that you don't need to meet your basic needs, but are fun to have. What luxury items are popular with your friends this year?

What Europeans Wanted

The main thing Europeans wanted to trade for was furs. Europeans made most of their warm clothing out of wool from sheep. Richer people, however, liked coats, trims, and hats made from fur. So furs such as lynx, fox, mink, and beaver were valuable **luxury** items in Europe.

Beaver hats weren't actually made from beaver fur. They were made from **felt**. Felt was made by scraping off the fine **under fur** from the beaver skin, then wetting and crushing it until it was matted together. This made a material something like thick, wet cardboard. This was then dried and shaped into hats.

Some Aboriginal groups made beaver coats with the fur on the inside. After a year or two, the outer hairs wore off and the under fur was matted. This was perfect for making felt, so these old coats were valuable to Europeans!

The Wellington (1812)

The Paris Beau (1815)

The Regent (1825)

The D'Orsay (1820)

Beavers were one of the game animals Aboriginal peoples traditionally hunted for food and clothing. Beavers have warm coats designed for cold climates. The under fur is thick. The long hairs of the outer fur trap warm air inside.

The most fashionable piece of clothing in Europe was a beaver hat. By the 1600s, though, there weren't many beavers left in Europe because of all the hunting for furs to make hats.

What Aboriginal Peoples Wanted

At first, Aboriginal peoples were most interested in trading for metal goods such as copper pots, knives, axe heads, and sewing needles. Once they understood how guns worked, these were highly prized, too.

These items helped Aboriginal peoples meet their basic needs. Once they had these things, they became interested in luxury items such as blankets, cloth, and beads. In time, they also came to like European foods such as biscuits and raisins. Later on, alcohol (brandy) and tobacco became important trade items.

Museums often display artifacts such as these trade items from the Hudson's Bay Company. What are the goods shown in this display?

Try This

Review the information about the goods Europeans offered in trade. Draw a picture of one of the tools Aboriginal peoples wanted. Write a caption to explain why you think it was useful. You might want to work in a group to make a "museum" display of trade goods.

Before you start, think about what you already know about traditional Aboriginal technology. You might need to review what you know about awls, cooking pots, knives, adzes, and weapons used by different groups.

The Colony of New France

Donnacona's people, the Haudenosaunee, no longer lived in the area. Historians think they might have been driven south during wars with another group in the area called the Algonquin [al-GONG-kwun].

*E*uropeans soon learned that if they got to Tadoussac in early spring they had the best choice of furs. Soon they decided to set up their own trading posts so that they could stay there all winter. Then they were sure to get the best furs.

Now the French king decided to try again to set up a colony along the St. Lawrence River. In 1608, a French map-maker and navigator named Samuel de Champlain [sham-PLANE] set up a colony close to where Donnacona's village had once been. They called their colony **Québec**.

The name *Québec* was the French version of the Algonquin word for "where the river narrows." This drawing was by the artist C.W. Jeffreys. In what way does Québec look like a Haudenosaunee village?

Champlain's Idea

The French wanted the top-quality furs from the Subarctic region. But they didn't know where to go to get the furs or how to travel there. Champlain decided that they would have to learn from the Aboriginal peoples. He hoped to find a way to fit into the **trade network** that linked Aboriginal groups from many different regions.

Getting Along

One of the first things Champlain did was to arrange an **exchange**. A 17-year-old French boy called Étienne Brulé [ay-TYEN broo-LAY] went to live with the Algonquin and then the Wendat [WEN-dat] to learn their language and customs. At the same time, a Wendat boy called Savignon [sa-vee-NOH(N)] went with Champlain on a trip to France.

Étienne Brulé grew to love the Wendat way of life. He returned to Québec only to help out Champlain and the fur traders.

Savignon wasn't as happy in France. He reported back that this was a strange place where children were treated badly. There were beggars everywhere and people argued loudly in the streets. Savignon was very glad to come home!

Today, young people often go on exchange programs. They live with other families in different parts of Canada or even different parts of the world. How do you think this might help people understand one another?

When you look at this map, it might seem easy to see where to go to get furs. But the French saw only the forests and lakes and rivers. They didn't have any maps to show them where to go.

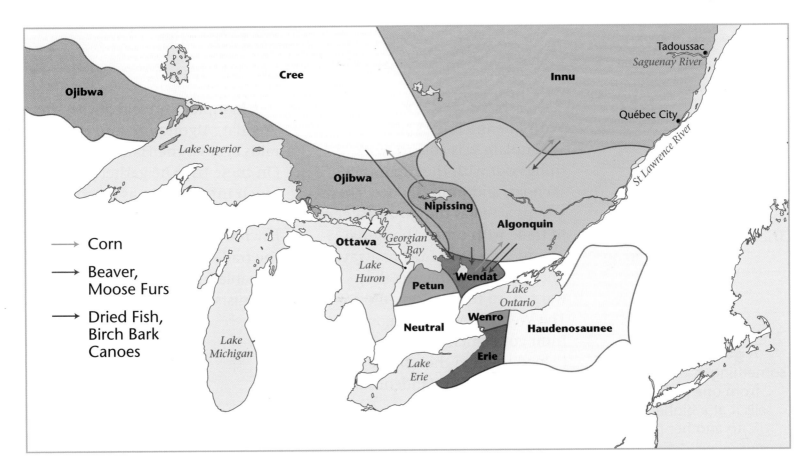

Corn

Beaver, Moose Furs

Dried Fish, Birch Bark Canoes

When the French first arrived, the Wendat were the most powerful traders in the area. In this picture, women are pounding corn into grain in tubs made out of hollow tree trunks. The men are getting ready to go trading.

A **go-between** buys something at a low price from one person and sells it at a higher price to another person.

The Idea Works

With Étienne Brulé's help, Champlain was able to work things out with the Algonquin, Wendat, and Innu [IN-oo]. These groups acted as the **go-betweens** in trade with other Aboriginal groups who lived further away. The French got the furs they wanted, so their colony did well. The Wendat, Algonquin, and Innu got French guns, which helped them in their battles with their enemy, the Haudenosaunee.

Champlain travelled with the Wendat, Algonquin, and Innu on raids against the Haudenosaunee. On these trips he gathered as much information as he could. He made maps of the St. Lawrence area and learned how the trade routes worked. This was valuable information for the colonists.

A Closer Look

Some Aboriginal Traders

The Wendat and Haudenosaunee

The traditional territories of the Wendat and the Haudenosaunee are around the Great Lakes in the Eastern Woodlands region. Although the Wendat and Haudenosaunee were enemies, their cultures were similar. Both lived year-round in villages made up of wooden longhouses. (Turn to page 139 to see this type of village.) Women and girls grew corn, beans, and squash and collected wild plants. Men and boys hunted, fished, and traded.

In the past, the Wendat were called the *Huron* [HYUR-on]. The Haudenosaunee were called the *Iroquois* [IR-uh-kwah].

At the time of contact with Europeans, the people of the Great Lakes area were the only Aboriginal groups in Canada who made pottery. This pot is about 500 years old.

The Innu

The Innu's traditional territories are in the Subarctic region. Their way of life was similar to other Subarctic hunters, such as the Dunne-za. In the past, the Innu nearest the St. Lawrence area were called the *Montagnais* [mon-tuh-NYAY].

These Innu moccasins are made from sealskin dyed with spruce roots.

The Algonquin

The traditional territories of the Algonquin are on the border between the Eastern Woodlands and the Subarctic region. Some Algonquin groups traditionally lived by hunting. Others also grew corn, beans, and squash.

This Algonquin birch bark container shows how people decorated their everyday objects.

REAL PEOPLE: SAMUEL DE CHAMPLAIN (C. 1570–1635)

Samuel de Champlain set up the colony of New France. He worked hard for many years to keep peoples' spirits up and to get money from France to keep things going. He also got along with the Aboriginal peoples in the area, which made things easier for the colonists.

Champlain was a skilled map-maker. He also kept careful notes and drawings of the people, animals, plants, and places he saw on his travels. He was an expert navigator—he crossed the Atlantic 23 times during his life!

We don't know much about Champlain's personal life. He was married, but his wife didn't like life in the colony and returned to France.

By the time he died in 1635, Champlain knew he had gotten the colony of New France off to a good start.

Think For Yourself

Think back to the adventures of Jacques Cartier. In what way did Champlain have similar goals? What did the two men do differently? You might want to discuss your ideas with a partner. You could use a Venn diagram or another kind of chart to compare the two explorers.

Coureurs de Bois

At first the French relied on Aboriginal groups to bring them furs. As they learned more about the area, however, they realized they could buy furs for less if they travelled to the people who actually trapped the animals. This cut out the go-betweens.

The young men who set out to trade on their own were called *coureurs de bois* [koo-RUR-duh-BWAH], which means "runners of the woods." They learned to live off the land in the same way as Aboriginal peoples did.

Coureurs de bois set out by canoe in the summer. Sometimes they spent the winter in Aboriginal communities and returned to the colony in the spring. Other times they travelled "round trip" during the summer. They tried to travel in groups of three so that they had help if something went wrong.

This way of trading worked well for the Europeans. It became the way things were done in the fur trade for almost 300 years.

Women in the Fur Trade

The *coureurs de bois* got along well with Aboriginal peoples because they married Aboriginal women.

The *coureurs de bois* bought the furs at a low price from Aboriginal communities, then sold them to merchants at a higher price. The merchants then shipped them to France and sold them for an even higher price!

Here are some of the things these traders are loading into their canoe: corn meal, pemmican, a canvas tarp to use as a tent or a sail, ammunition, and trade goods. They are also taking a canoe repair kit of spruce roots, pitch, and bark.

This meant they became part of the communities they traded with. The wives taught the *coureurs de bois* the local language and helped them understand the culture. They were also their work partners.

Women often went on trading trips. They had many jobs. They made the food, set up the camp, carried goods around rapids, and mended clothing and canoes.

Try This

Draw a picture to show one thing *coureurs de bois* learned from Aboriginal peoples. This might be a tool or a way of doing something. Write a caption that explains what you know about this and why you think *coureurs de bois* chose the Aboriginal way.

You might want to work in a group to make a display of Aboriginal tools and ways of doing things that were used by the Europeans. (You'll find more information about winter travel in the next section, "More Exploration.")

More Exploration

Over the next 200 years, Europeans spent as much time fighting each other over trade as they did finding furs!

The Trade Wars

For a long time the competition over trade was between the French and the English. The English had set up colonies to the north and south of the French. Both sides wanted to get the most—and the best—furs and to control the fur trade.

In 1763, the English took over New France. Now the competition over trade was between two companies: the Hudson's Bay Company and the North West Company. For many years they fought each other as they searched for the best furs. Traders attacked one another. Sometimes people were killed.

In 1821, the two companies joined forces. Then things finally settled down.

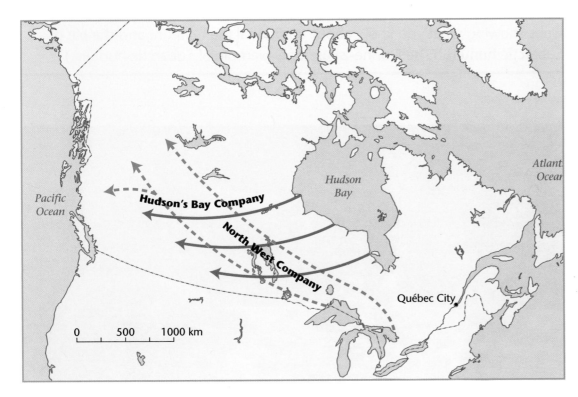

During the years of the trade wars, the fur trade gradually moved west.

Exploring

During the trade wars, the fur-trading companies paid for explorers to go with Aboriginal guides into new areas. There were three main reasons for this:

- Europeans were *still* looking for the Northwest Passage to the Pacific Ocean.

- The fur traders could get furs more cheaply if they didn't buy them from Aboriginal go-betweens.

- After awhile, most of the animals near the forts had been hunted and killed, so they needed to find new areas to get furs.

In the rest of this section, you can find out about a trip made between 1770 and 1772 by a Chipewyan [chi-puh-WY-un] leader called Matonabbee [mat-uh-NAH-bee] and an English explorer called Samuel Hearne. They travelled together through the Subarctic and into the Arctic. This is one example of how Europeans and Aboriginal peoples worked together to explore.

The Chipewyan and the Cree were two Aboriginal groups who were important trading partners for the Hudson's Bay Company.

Try This

Before you read about Matonabbee and Samuel Hearne, make webs showing what you know about the Subarctic and Arctic environments. Make two more webs showing what you know about traditional Inuit culture and the life of Subarctic hunters. (The Dunne-za are one example of Subarctic hunters.)

This shows the Coppermine River near where it flows into the Arctic Ocean.

Journey to the North

Samuel Hearne worked for the Hudson's Bay Company. Most of what we know about the trip he made with Matonabbee comes from a book he wrote about his adventures.

What region did Samuel Hearne explore in 1770 to1772?

Samuel Hearne explored the region between Fort Prince of Wales on Hudson Bay and the Coppermine River where it flows into the Arctic Ocean.

What was Hearne looking for?

Hearne was looking for a large river and a copper mine. Three years before some Chipewyan traders had brought large lumps of raw copper to the fort. They told of a great river that led to the sea. The Hudson's Bay Company hoped this was the Northwest Passage, or at least that its ships could travel up the river and bring back copper.

Hearne had tried to find the river and the mines in 1769 and 1770. Both of these trips ended before they had gone far. On his first trip, Hearne was robbed and deserted by his guides. He was lucky to get back to the fort alive!

Who showed Hearne the way?

At the end of Hearne's second trip he met a Chipewyan leader called Matonabbee. Once again, Hearne's guides had robbed him of most of his goods, and he was very cold in his European clothing. Matonabbee gave Hearne a warm suit made from otter skins to keep out the cold. He probably saved Hearne's life.

Reading Hint

This section uses questions to organize the investigation. The questions are headings.

Matonabbee was part Cree and part Chipewyan. He was a respected Elder and trader. Hearne described Matonabbee as "the most sociable, kind, and sensible Indian I had ever met with. He was a man well known and generally respected."

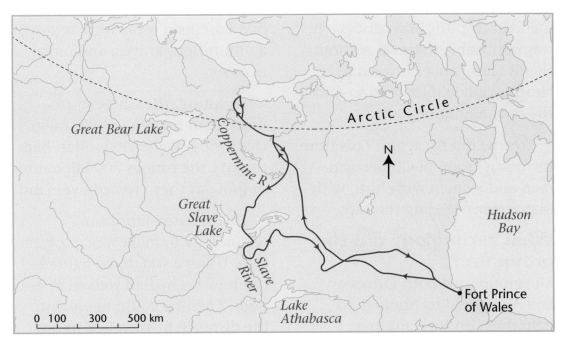

0 100   300   500 km

The map shows Samuel Hearne's journey in 1770.

Fort Prince of Wales was built in 1718. It was an unusual fort because the walls were built of stone, 11 to 12 metres thick and 5 metres high. Most forts were made of wood. This drawing is by Samuel Hearne.

One woman had a baby during the trip. The group stopped for a couple of days when the baby was born. Then the baby joined the party and they all moved on!

When he learned how badly Hearne's trip had gone, Matonabbee told him it was because he had poor guides. He also told him it was a mistake not to take women on the trip. He explained that women carried supplies, prepared food, and mended clothing and canoes—it was impossible to travel without them! Matonabbee offered to be Hearne's guide if he tried to find the river and mines again.

Hearne did try again. This time he took a group of Chipewyan men and women with him, with Matonabbee leading the way.

What technology did the group use?

The group used both European and Aboriginal technology to help them on their journey.

Women carried most of the goods and usually pulled the **toboggans**. (Sometimes dogs helped, too.) The group slept in deerskin tents on part of the journey. Other times they slept in the open or in the shelter of rocks or snow banks. The group also had European tools such as guns, ammunition, knives, and metal needles.

In spring, the Chipewyan made light canoes to help them cross wide rivers. They often had to carry the canoes 200 kilometres or more as they crossed over land.

Hearne used European technology to make a map of the area. Using a watch, he figured out how far he had walked in one hour. Then he could figure out the distance he travelled in one

This is what the group might have looked like when they set out in December. The sleds used by the Chipewyan did not have runners. They are called *toboggans*. What Aboriginal technologies do you see? What are the European technologies?

day. Hearne used a compass to tell him what direction he was travelling in. He also used a quadrant to check his location, the same way a sailor would.

What were some of the challenges they faced?

The two main challenges for the group were finding food and surviving the cold weather. In his book, Hearne tells of daily adventures. You can read about some of them here.

The group left Fort Prince of Wales in the snow and cold on 7 December 1770. Soon they reached the place where Matonabbee had left a cache of food, but it had been stolen!

From the nineteenth we traversed nothing but entirely barren ground, *with empty bellies, till the twenty-seventh.*

On December 27th, they came across a herd of caribou. Matonabbee told Hearne that they would travel with the caribou herd to make sure they always had enough food. This was the traditional way for the Chipewyan to meet their basic needs.

Hearne got used to the cold weather, but some days were worse than others. On February 7th, they crossed a lake that was about 22 kilometres wide.

It is impossible to describe the intenseness of the cold this day. We [crossed] in two hours, though several of the women who were heavy laden took much longer. Several of the Indians were much frozen.

What do you think it would be like to walk in the snow for eight days without any food?

Hearne was 24 years old when he made this trip. He later became an important person in the Hudson's Bay Company and set up the fort of Cumberland House. He married a woman named Mary Norton, who was part English and part Cree.

Why do you think the Chipewyan would leave a sick person behind? What would happen if the whole group stopped to wait for someone to get better?

Towards the end of April, the group was travelling at half their normal speed. This time it was because the weather was too warm!

The weather was in general so hot, and so much snow had been melted, it [was] bad walking in snowshoes, and heavy hauling.

They reached the Coppermine River in July. Hearne was surprised that the river was so shallow. They looked for copper, but only found small amounts.

They soon started the journey home. The Chipewyan were in a hurry to get back, so they walked many kilometres every day. Hearne's feet became very sore. He had to keep going, though, because it was the Chipewyan custom to leave behind anyone who wasn't well enough to travel.

My feet and legs had swelled considerably. The nails of my toes were bruised to such a degree that several of them fell off. The skin was entirely chafed off from the tops of both my feet, and between every toe. For a whole day I left the print of my feet in blood almost at every step I took.

Samuel Hearne's feet healed, but it took six more months of walking to get back to Fort Prince of Wales!

What did Hearne find out?

- He found out that a river led into the Arctic Ocean, but it was not large and there were no great copper mines.

- He collected enough information to make a map that other Europeans could use to find their way in the area.

- He recorded information about plants and animals in the region.

- He recorded information about the ways in which the Chipewyan and other groups lived.

Think For Yourself

Imagine you could travel back in time to interview Samuel Hearne, Matonabbee, or a member of their group for your television program *Great Adventures*. You'd like to talk to them about what happened on their trip and how they felt about it.

Decide who to interview, then make a list of three to five questions to ask. You might want to work in a group. You could then select members of your group to be the interviewer, the guest, and the audience. After the interview, you could invite the audience to ask questions.

 **Do an Interview**

Get organized before you start! Think about what you want to know. *Who, What, Where, When, Why,* and *How* are the questions newspaper reporters use to make sure they get all the information they need. Here are some other hints for successful interviews.

1. Brainstorm what you'd like to find out, then pick three to five of your best questions.

2. When you ask questions, pay attention to the answers. Nod to show you are listening. Don't interrupt.

3. Sometimes ask for more information. Try *"Tell me more about ..."* and *"How did you feel when ...."*

Find Out

Research and report on a journey made by these European explorers: Alexander Mackenzie, Simon Fraser, or David Thompson. You might use the questions about Samuel Hearne in this section to focus your research. You might have other questions you want to investigate. Remember to include Aboriginal peoples' points of view.

Think of a creative way to report your findings. For example, you could role-play an Aboriginal woman telling what the trip was like for her. Or you could write a journal entry describing where the explorer went and what he found.

Looking Back

In this chapter, you discovered how Aboriginal peoples and Europeans worked together in the fur trade and to explore. You also saw how to use questions to organize an investigation.

Why is asking questions an important part of social studies?

Chapter 10

Contact and Change

Get ready to practise your bargaining skills!

From 1600 to 1900, the fur trade was an important part of life in Canada. During this time, the fur trade created a way of life that had many benefits for both Aboriginal peoples and European merchants. At first, Europeans had to fit into Aboriginal ways of doing things. In time, though, Aboriginal peoples found that contact with Europeans caused many changes to their cultures.

In this chapter, you can learn more about how the fur trade worked and find out what trade items were important in British Columbia. You can also investigate some of the challenges that Aboriginal peoples faced as their lands became the country called Canada.

Exchanging Goods

There are two main ways of exchanging goods: **bartering** and **buying and selling**. When you barter, you trade one thing for another. When you buy and sell, you give someone money. In return, that person gives you what you want.

Bargaining

In the fur trade, Aboriginal traders and European merchants bartered for goods. Furs were exchanged for goods from Europe. The merchants kept records of the prices paid for certain goods, but **bargaining** was always possible.

In bargaining, the buyer tries to pay the lowest price. The seller tries to get the highest price. A hunter could argue that his furs were of a high quality and so were worth more. A merchant could argue that there were many furs this year so he could pay less to somebody else. In the end, they might agree on a price somewhere in the middle.

Trading Customs

To trade with Aboriginal groups, Europeans had to learn Aboriginal trading customs. Trading could take place when a trader visited an Aboriginal community, or when Aboriginal people came to a trading post.

In most Aboriginal communities there was a **trading captain**. This person spoke for the group. He played an important role in the ceremonies and watched over all the trading to make sure everything was done fairly. In many communities, though, women did the actual bargaining.

What other reasons do you think a trader could give for getting a higher price? What reasons could a merchant give for a lower price?

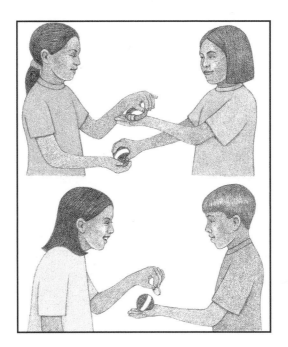

Which people are bartering and which are buying and selling? What is one thing that is the same in these two ways of exchanging goods? What is one thing that is different?

A **made beaver** was a top-quality beaver pelt. Sometimes the Hudson's Bay Company gave out tokens that could be used later in trade at the trading post. In what way were these tokens like money? In what way were they not?

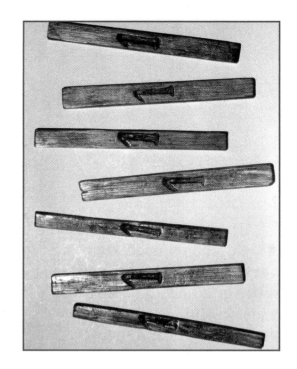

Sample Prices
11 made beaver = 1 gun
2 made beaver = 1 axe
2 made beaver = 1 black fox fur
1 made beaver = 5 fish hooks
1 made beaver = 2 white fox furs
1 made beaver = 9 martin furs

In The Words Of...

Charles Lalemant

This description was written by a European priest, Charles Lalemant (sharl LA-luh-mah(n)], in 1626. It describes trading between the French and a group of Aboriginal peoples. These customs remained the same for most of the fur trade.

When you read this, notice that the writer calls Aboriginal peoples "Indians." Why do you think he did this? Think back to what you know about Christopher Columbus.

The day of their arrival [the French merchants] erect their huts and the Indians arrive in their canoes.

The second day the Indians hold a council and present their gifts. Gifts are always given when people visit each other. The French give presents then to the Indians.

The third and fourth day the Indians trade and barter their furs for blankets, hatchets, kettles, capes, little glass beads, and many similar things. It is a pleasure to watch them during this trading.

When it is over they take one more day for the feast which is made for them, and the dance. Early the next morning the Indians disappear like a flock of birds.

The Jesuit Relations.

Think For Yourself

Work in partners to role-play trading. Decide who will be an Aboriginal trading captain and who will be a merchant. Follow the ceremonies for trading and try to get the best price you can for your side. Then switch sides.

After you have finished role-playing, write a journal entry from the point of view of either a trading captain or a merchant. Explain why you want furs or why you want European goods.

Voyageurs

Voyageurs worked for the big fur-trading companies. They took trade goods to Aboriginal communities and brought back furs. *Voyageurs* were proud of their ability to paddle large trading canoes all day and carry heavy loads around rapids.

This painting of *voyageurs* [voy-uh-ZHURZ] is by Frances Ann Hopkins. Her husband worked for the Hudson's Bay Company. She made many trips with *voyageurs*.

The Métis

The fur trade created a whole new culture in North America: the **Métis** [may-TEE]. The Métis are people of mixed Aboriginal and European heritage. The first Métis were the children of Aboriginal women and European traders. Later, many Métis worked as *voyageurs*.

The fur trade required a great deal of pemmican to feed travellers. Métis communities supplied much of this. They traded buffalo pemmican for other goods they wanted.

This shows a Métis camp preparing for a buffalo hunt. They organized great buffalo hunts twice a year. Many Métis lived on farms.

Find Out

Form a group to put on a "talk show" in which a group of Métis people discuss their parts in the fur trade. Your "guests" on the show could take on these roles: a buffalo hunt captain, a woman who makes pemmican, and a *voyageur*. Prepare for the show by researching each of these roles.

Otters, Beavers, and Salmon

The fur trade got to British Columbia almost 200 years after it first started in Tadoussac on the St. Lawrence. It took the explorers longer to get here because this part of North America is the furthest from Europe.

Many parts of the fur trade were the same in British Columbia as in other places, but some things were different. The big difference was that beaver wasn't always the most important trade item.

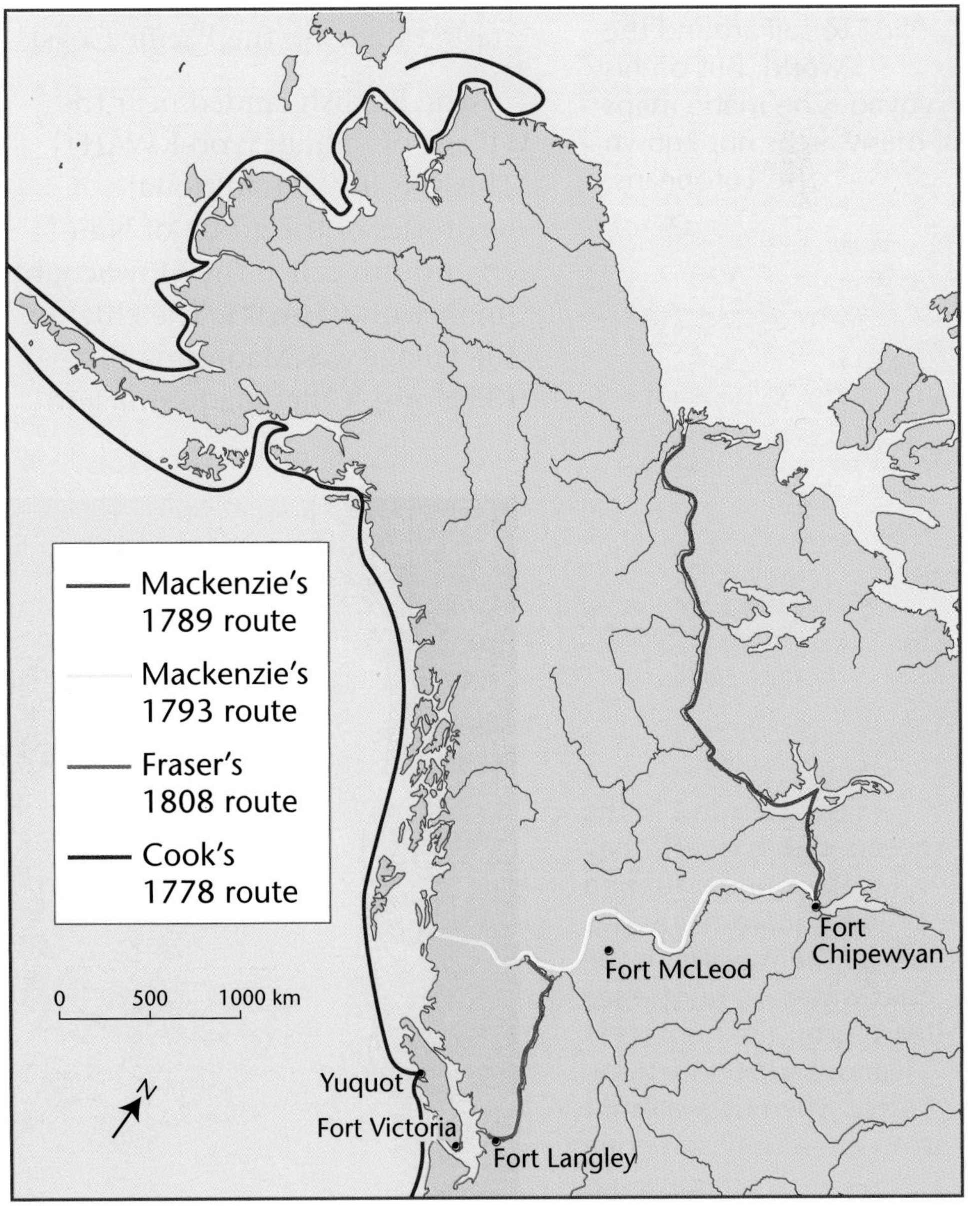

This map shows you explorers' routes and some of the places you can read about in this section.

Mackenzie's 1789 route

Mackenzie's 1793 route

Fraser's 1808 route

Cook's 1778 route

0   500   1000 km

Yuquot

Fort Victoria

Fort Langley

Fort McLeod

Fort Chipewyan

Captain Cook was one of the greatest explorers of his time. He wasn't the first to sail around the world, but on his voyages he made maps of many areas not known to Europeans.

The Sea Otter Trade

In 1778, two English ships, led by Captain James Cook, arrived at the coast of British Columbia. Cook and his crew were trying to find the Northwest Passage from the Pacific side. It had been a long journey. They had sailed from England around the bottom of Africa, and then across the Pacific Ocean. Spanish sailors had made the trip a few years earlier. It was Cook's visit, though, that really started trade on the Pacific Coast.

The English landed near the village of Yuquot [yoo-KWAHT]. This was in the traditional territories of the group of Nuu-chah-nulth called the Mowachaht [moh-wuh-CHAHT]. The chief in the village was Maquinna [ma-KEEN-uh]. Chief Maquinna and his people welcomed the English—even though at first they thought they might be the spirits of fish in human form because they were so pale!

The English stayed for a month to repair their ships. During this time, the Mowachaht and the English traded many goods. One thing Europeans got in trade were **sea otter** furs.

On their way back to Europe, the English visited China. There they discovered that they could get a lot of money for sea otter furs. At the time, they didn't know this in Europe. When they found out, the sea otter trade became big business. By 1792, many ships were calling at villages up and down the Pacific Coast each year.

Sea otters live in the ocean. Like beavers, they have thick under fur and long guard hairs. This keeps them warm in the cold water. To hunt a sea otter, a group of hunters in canoes surrounded the otter. Then they all shot arrows at it until someone made a hit.

One purpose of Cook's voyages was to collect information about people, plants, and animals around the world. John Webber was the artist who recorded what they saw. This is Webber's drawing of the English ships at Yuquot.

Fur Trade by Land

The people of the Subarctic region of BC first came in contact with Europeans in 1793. This is when the explorer Alexander Mackenzie travelled through their lands.

Mackenzie was making a long journey from the east to the Pacific Ocean. On the last part of his journey he was guided by the Dunne-za [duh-ne-ZAH], Sekani [sik-AN-ee], Wet'suwet'en [wet-SOO-wet-en], Dakelh [da-KEL], Nuxalk [nu-HALK], and Heiltsuk [HILE-tsuk]. For Mackenzie, it was a great adventure in an unknown land. For the Aboriginal peoples, it was just another trip along the **Grease Trail**.

Later, another explorer named Simon Fraser travelled through the area. After that, the first North West Company fort was set up at McLeod Lake. This was in 1805. The Subarctic was rich in beaver, as well as other game, so there were many furs to trade.

Aboriginal peoples usually welcomed forts being set up in their territories because they could be the go-betweens in trade with other groups. By the 1830s, there were several forts all through the Interior, and there was much trading.

Fort Langley

One fur-trading fort that didn't work out the way the Europeans planned was Fort Langley. This fort was built in Stó:lō territories in 1827. The Stó:lō didn't want to

Traders called the Aboriginal peoples who moved to live near forts the **home guard**. These people brought in furs from other groups. They also supplied trading forts with meat and fish to eat.

The Grease Trail was the main trade route in the area between the Pacific Coast and the Interior. Eulachon oil (grease) was an important trade item.

change their way of life to spend more time trapping animals for the fur trade. They wanted to fish as they had always done.

At first the European traders were disappointed. Then they realized how many salmon there were in the area and how good they were to eat. Salmon became a valuable resource. The traders began shipping the fish to Europe and other places.

Fort Langley was built like most fur-trading forts. How would you describe it?

Think For Yourself

Here's a BIG QUESTION about the fur trade that you could discuss in a group:

- *Based on what you know, do you think Aboriginal peoples chose to be part of the fur trade, or did they have to be part of it once the Europeans came? Why do you think this?*

Here are some SMALL QUESTIONS to get you thinking:

- *What might have happened if Aboriginal peoples had not brought furs to the forts or the sailing ships?*
- *What might have happened if some groups traded and others did not?*

Find Out

Do some research to find out more about trading forts near your community. Before you start, focus your research. Think about BIG and SMALL questions that would help you to understand what went on at the fort. Remember to consider the European and the Aboriginal points of view about trade in the area.

When Cultures Change

All cultures change a little over time. For example, you might know that fashion and music were different when your parents were young than they are now. These are small changes in culture.

Some events cause big changes to a culture, though. For Aboriginal peoples, European technologies and the fur trade changed some of the ways they did things. Other things that came with the fur trade caused even bigger changes. These things were diseases, missionaries, and European settlement.

Diseases

Aboriginal peoples had no **resistance** to European diseases. Once European diseases got into an Aboriginal community, many, and sometimes most, of the people died. This is called an **epidemic**.

Missionaries

Missionaries [MISH-uh-nair-eez] were Europeans who came to Canada to teach Aboriginal peoples about Christianity. They also set up schools to teach Aboriginal children to read and write European languages. They tried to convince Aboriginal peoples that their beliefs and traditions were wrong.

Settlers

In time, many Europeans decided to live in North America. They took over the traditional territories of Aboriginal peoples for their farms and towns. When this happened, the Aboriginal peoples had to move to smaller areas of land called **reserves**.

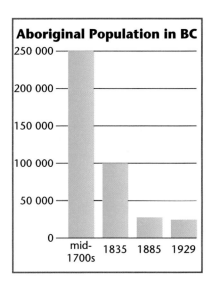

Aboriginal Population in BC

A **bar graph** is one way to compare numbers. What numbers does this bar graph compare? What can you figure out if you know that large smallpox epidemics happened around 1800, near 1840, and in the 1860s? (Figure out where these dates fit on the graph.)

Resistance is what makes your body able to fight off disease. The disease that caused the most deaths was **smallpox**. People with smallpox get sores all over their bodies and high fevers.

Think For Yourself

What are your first ideas about the changes that disease, missionaries, and settlers might have caused in Aboriginal communities? Make a few notes. You can check your ideas after you read the next section, "Facing Challenges."

Facing Challenges

In this section, you can find out about the challenges Aboriginal peoples faced because of contact with Europeans. Most of this information is about Chief Maquinna's people, the Mowachaht.

All across Canada, Aboriginal groups first benefitted from the fur trade. Then they faced hard times when the fur traders moved to find new trading partners. The story of the Mowachaht is just one example.

To make sure we make things better in the future, it is important to understand some of the challenges people faced in the past.

Good Times

The beginning of the sea otter trade was good for Chief Maquinna and his people. There were plenty of sea otters and Europeans paid a high price for their furs. The Mowachaht sold the furs they got. They also acted as go-betweens for other groups who did not live near the coast.

REAL PEOPLE: CHIEF MAQUINNA

Maquinna is an ancestral name of the Mowachaht. The Chief Maquinna who welcomed Captain Cook was the man who had the name and the rights and honours that went with it at that time. A Spanish priest who visited the area around the same time drew this picture of Maquinna. It shows him wearing the special whaler's hat that only chiefs could wear.

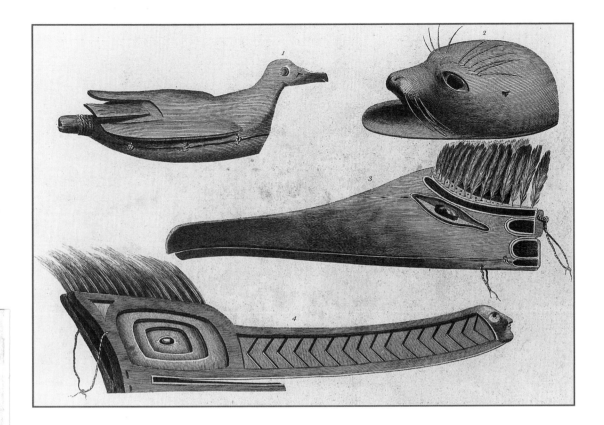

These drawings of Nuu-chah-nulth masks were made by Captain Cook's artist, John Webber. The masks were carved out of cedar. Can you spot the sea otter?

The goods the Mowachaht got in exchange for furs made parts of their lives easier. For example, it was easier to cook in a copper pot than to heat rocks. They also enjoyed luxury items. For example, sometimes they cut up pots to make bracelets.

Maquinna became a more important chief because of all the wealth he got from trading. He added to his name by giving huge potlatches where he gave away European goods such as blankets and clothing.

European goods also helped Aboriginal artists. Metal tools made it easier to carve, and many beautiful works were created. Coastal communities carved more totem poles than before. Artists also started making smaller works to trade with Europeans.

New Ways

It wasn't long before the people of Yuquot spent most of their time working in the sea otter trade. They either hunted for sea otters, traded with other groups to get furs, or fought to protect their trading spots.

People were so busy with the sea otter trade that they didn't have time to harvest resources in the traditional ways. Soon the Mowachaht came to depend on European goods to meet their basic needs. They started to use flour, for example, in their cooking. Because they traded away so many furs, they

This photograph of a coastal community was taken in 1899. The people have gathered for a potlatch. Can you see the big pile of blankets? What traditional ways of doing things do you see in this photograph? What new ways do you see?

depended on European blankets to keep warm.

Another change was that wars between groups along the coast became more dangerous. Many more people were killed with guns than with the traditional weapons of arrows and clubs. At one time Chief Maquinna had an army of 300 to 400 men.

Smallpox

The first smallpox epidemic to hit Nuu-chah-nulth territories was in 1804. By the 1860s, half the people in the area had died. Along the coast, whole villages disappeared.

Many Elders died, so there were few people left to pass on their history. Many stories and customs were lost. People also lost

Today, we have **vaccinations** to fight diseases like smallpox. These "shots" make sure your body can resist certain diseases.

faith in their beliefs. This was partly because the Christian missionaries told them that their beliefs were wrong. It was also partly because shamans could not protect the people from the smallpox epidemics.

No More Sea Otters

The Mowachaht wanted to get as many furs as possible. They hunted all the animals they could find, not just those they needed to meet their basic needs. By 1840, there weren't many sea otters left in the area.

The European traders figured out how to get to other groups who still had furs. Now the ships no longer stopped at Yuquot and the Mowachaht lost their jobs as go-betweens.

When Maquinna's people no longer had any furs to trade, they were in trouble. They had changed their way of life. Now they *needed* European goods, but they had nothing to trade for them. Even if they wanted to return to the traditional ways, they couldn't. So many people had died from diseases that there weren't enough people left to do the work.

Settlers

In 1849, Vancouver Island became a colony of England. The capital was Fort Victoria. This meant many settlers arrived who wanted to own land. Aboriginal peoples were forced to move onto reserves.

At first, the Mowachaht lands were too far away from Victoria to interest anyone. After awhile, though, the Mowachaht also had to move onto reserves.

The reserve lands were not big enough to provide all the resources the Mowachaht needed. There were also new laws about fishing and chopping down trees. By 1900, life for the Mowachaht was very hard. Many people were poor and hungry, and they were often sick.

In time, sea otters became **extinct** on the BC coast—they were all killed. Wildlife experts brought sea otters from the United States to British Columbia. Slowly, the number of sea otters in BC is growing again.

Try This

Describe one way each of these events changed Mowachaht life. These could be changes for the better, or changes for the worse.

- the fur trade

- European technologies

- European diseases

- missionaries

- European settlement

Fight or Negotiate?

A treaty is an agreement between two groups of people. Negotiating is like bargaining. For awhile, the government gave each of the main treaties a number. There were 11 of these treaties altogether.

Louis Riel [loo-EE ree-EL] was a Métis leader who believed his people had the right to form their own country. He led fights against the government in 1869 and 1884. He was arrested and hanged for this in 1885.

After awhile, Aboriginal peoples realized that contact with Europeans had caused things to change for the worse. So many people had died of diseases they didn't have much power. Still, some tried to fight. Others tried to **negotiate treaties**.

Fight

When Aboriginal peoples fought, the governments they fought against saw them as criminals. They didn't see them as people of one nation defending their rights against another nation. So when they lost, they were punished like criminals.

There were many small fights in different parts of British Columbia. One of the biggest events happened in 1864. Some European miners and settlers were building a road through the Tsilhqot'in [tsil-KOH-tin] lands in the Interior. The settlers had already taken over some land. The Tsilhqot'in didn't want to lose any more land because they were afraid they wouldn't be able to meet their basic needs. So a group of Tsilhquot'in people killed 13 of the miners and settlers. The leaders of the group were captured and hanged.

At times, there were fights between the crews of trading ships and villagers along the coast. Sometimes the traders started it. Other times the villagers started it. None of these battles ever became very big, though.

Negotiate

In some areas, Aboriginal groups negotiated treaties with the government. The idea was that the treaties would give Aboriginal peoples lands and other rights that were theirs. Settlers would have the rest of the land. Many Aboriginal leaders worked hard to protect the rights of their people through these treaties.

In British Columbia between 1851 and 1854, the government of the colony negotiated treaties with some groups on Vancouver Island. (These treaties were not numbered.) In 1899, the Sekani, Dunne-za, and Dene-thah [de-ney-TA] became part of Treaty 8 with other Subarctic groups.

Aboriginal groups in other parts of the province kept asking the government to negotiate with them, too. But the government put off making any decisions.

Chief Crowfoot advised his people to sign Treaty 7 instead of fighting the settlers. The Siskasa [sis-KAH-suh] are Plains people who traditionally followed the buffalo herds. They agreed to move onto reserves in exchange for help setting up farms and ranches.

Find Out

Do a research project to find out more about Louis Riel or Chief Crowfoot. Use one of these BIG QUESTIONS to focus your research.

- *Was Riel a hero or a traitor?*
- *Did Crowfoot make the right decision when he signed Treaty 7?*

Looking Back

In this chapter, you saw how trade worked between Aboriginal peoples and European merchants. You also looked at some of the challenges Aboriginal peoples faced after contact with Europeans.

How do you think studying the events of the past can help us understand the issues in our communities today?

Chapter 11

Today and Tomorrow

This book is all about *beginnings*.

A lot of the information in this book is about the past. Investigating our beginnings in the past can help us understand the way things are today. Today is another type of beginning—the beginning of the future.

In this chapter, you can find out how people are working today to make sure we treat people of all cultures fairly. Some of this work is taking place in our governments. Some of it is being done by people in our communities.

You're part of this. It's your job to:

- Decide what needs to be done.
- Get out and do it!

How the BC Government Works

The government of British Columbia is powerful! It is made up of a few people who make decisions for everybody else. These decisions affect many parts of your life.

For example, the government of British Columbia decides what you learn in school and whether or not a forest will become a park. It also makes laws like the one that says you have to wear a helmet when you ride a bicycle.

The BIG QUESTION is: *Is it fair that a few people make all the decisions?*

In this section, you can find out how the government of British Columbia works. Then, you can decide for yourself if our type of government is fair.

In Victoria

In British Columbia, the government is made up of **Members of the Legislative Assembly (MLAs)**. MLAs are people from different parts of the province. They come together in Victoria, the capital of British Columbia, to discuss laws and make other decisions about how to run the province.

Voters

Voters are all the people in the province who are over 18 years old. Voting for a new government is called an **election**. The government must hold an election every five years. But it can hold one sooner if it wants.

During an election, **candidates** from different **political parties** make speeches explaining how they think the province should be run.

In Canada, the **federal government** makes laws all Canadians must follow. Each province and territory also has its own government. In a province, each community has another smaller government to take care of local matters.

A candidate is a person you can vote for in an election. A political party is a group of people with similar ideas.

This diagram shows the main parts of the BC government. Each part has different **responsibilities**. A responsibility is something that it is your job to do.

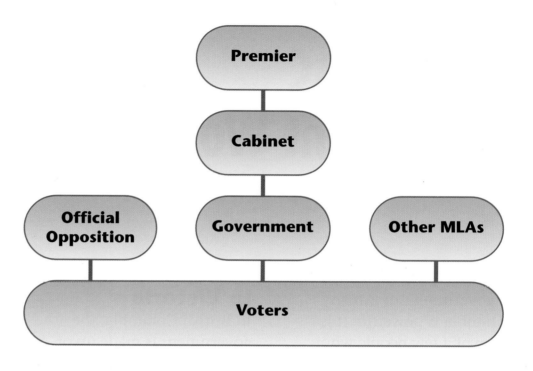

What qualities do you think a good MLA would have?

You don't have to be old enough to vote to write a letter to your MLA!

Each person votes for the candidate she or he likes best by marking an X beside that person's name on a piece of paper, then placing the vote into a box. It's the voters' responsibility to think about each candidate's point of view and decide which person they agree with.

After the election, everyone in the province must make sure they keep track of what the government is doing. People should let the government know whether or not they agree with its decisions by writing letters or phoning.

MLAs

The province is divided into 75 **ridings**. A riding includes one or more communities, depending on how many people live in the area.

The people in the riding get to elect one MLA.

At the end of election day, all the votes are counted. The candidate with the most votes wins. That person becomes the MLA for that riding. The MLA's responsibility is to find out what's important to the people in that riding and to make sure the government hears their ideas and opinions.

The Government

The political party with the most elected candidates forms the **government**. The leader of that political party becomes the **premier** of the province.

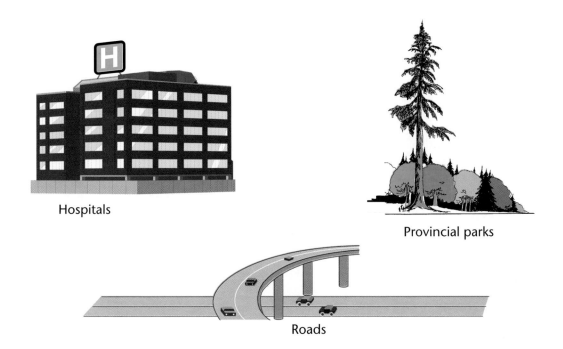

Hospitals

Provincial parks

Roads

The government must make sure the people of the province get the things they need, such as health care, roads, and a clean environment. Voters pay for this with their **taxes**—the money they must give the government each year.

The Official Opposition

The party that comes in second in an election forms the **Official Opposition**. The Official Opposition's responsibility is to say what it thinks about decisions the government makes. The Opposition often asks questions about the government's plans. MLAs from other political parties also ask the government questions.

The Cabinet

The **Cabinet** is made up of a group of government MLAs chosen by the premier. Each MLA in the Cabinet is a **minister** who is responsible for one area of government. For example, a minister of education is responsible for making sure that you receive a good education. A minister of the environment makes sure that we protect the land we live in.

It is the premier's job to decide how many ministers the government has and what their responsibilities are.

Making Laws

The Cabinet makes many important decisions about how to spend tax money. It can't make laws, though. To make a new law or change an old one, an MLA presents a **bill** in the Legislative Assembly. The bill explains the new law.

The issues are discussed. Then the MLAs vote on whether or not to make the bill a new law. If most MLAs vote "yes," then the bill becomes a law.

The MLAs meet at the Parliament Buildings in Victoria. The government sits on one side of the Assembly. The Official Opposition and other MLAs sit on the other side. The **Speaker** sits in the big chair at the front. The Speaker makes sure everyone has a chance to say what he or she thinks about an issue.

Try This

In a chart, list the responsibilities of the main parts of the BC government. Include:

- the people of British Columbia
- the MLAs
- the Cabinet
- the Official Opposition

You will probably have to skim pages 181 to 183 to find the information you need. Once you have collected the facts, decide on a type of chart that would show the information clearly.

Present your chart to the class. Give your opinion whether or not this system of government is fair to all people in the province. Explain your reasons.

Find Out

Find out who your local MLA is and what political party she or he belongs to. Write a letter to your MLA asking for her or his opinion on what the government can do to help people get along. Include your ideas about ways to help people in British Columbia get along.

Lessons from the Past

Today, the government of British Columbia is trying to find ways to make sure the rights of all people in the province are respected. This was not always true in the past.

For many years, the Canadian and British Columbian governments thought that the best way for people to get along was for everyone to be the same. They wanted Aboriginal peoples and new Canadians to give up their own cultures and become like Europeans.

What do you think of this idea?

Laws in the Past

The government did many things to try to change Aboriginal cultures. In British Columbia, for example, they passed a law that made potlatches illegal.

Another law said that all Aboriginal children had to go to **residential schools**. All across Canada, Aboriginal families had to send their children to live at schools run by people from European cultures. These schools were often far from the children's homes. At the schools, the

This picture shows boys at a residential school in their **dormitory** (where they slept.) What would it be like to be sent far from home and not be allowed to speak your own language?

children were not allowed to speak their own language or do the things that were normal in their culture.

Broken Cultures

Some Aboriginal people agreed with the government's ideas. Many others didn't. They tried to hide their children from people who came to take them away to school. In British Columbia, potlatches were sometimes held in secret. In the end, though, Aboriginal peoples didn't have enough power to change the government's ideas.

Because they could not practice their traditions, many Aboriginal communities began to have problems. The Elders could not show young people how to do things or tell them stories about the past because the children were away at the residential schools. Some young people didn't know what to do with their lives, and they got into trouble.

People's basic needs of food, clothing, and shelter were met, but they were losing other parts of their culture. Without all of the pieces, a culture has trouble surviving.

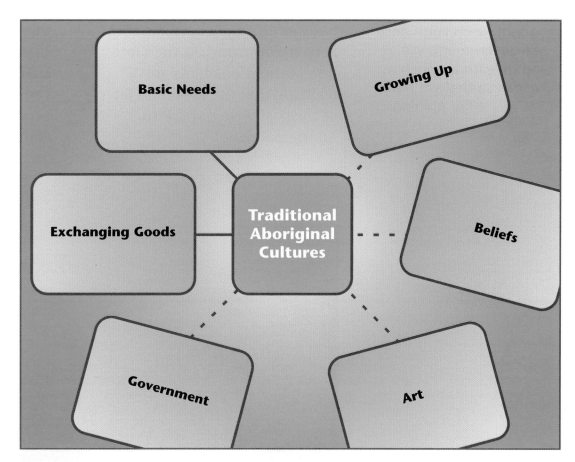

Think For Yourself

In a group, discuss the broken culture web. Try to imagine what happens when you take away one part of the web. After your discussion, decide how to complete this sentence:

• *A culture needs all of its parts because…*

New Ideas, New Challenges

Canadians have many different points of view about land claims and self-government. We all need to learn as much as we can so that we have fair opinions.

Today, many Aboriginal people are working to bring back the traditions of their cultures and keep them strong. At the same time, other Canadians are realizing that the ideas and laws of the past were not fair to Aboriginal peoples.

Two challenges for the future are **land claims** and **self-government**.

Land Claims

Land claims involve Aboriginal peoples' rights to certain lands. Some Aboriginal groups did not

During treaty negotiations, Nisga'a leaders arrived at the Parliament Buildings in a ceremonial canoe. Why do you think the Nisga'a chose to arrive in a traditional way?

sign treaties with the Canadian or provincial governments. These groups say they have never given up their rights to their traditional territories. They think it is time to start negotiating for this land.

The **Supreme Court** of Canada makes important decisions about laws in the country. The judges in the Supreme Court looked at this issue and at Canadian laws. They decided that Aboriginal peoples are right. Groups who have not signed treaties have rights to their traditional territories.

In 1998, the government of British Columbia began negotiating with Aboriginal groups in the province who did not already have treaties. These new treaties are different from the treaties in the past. They show more respect for the rights of Aboriginal peoples.

Self-government

Since 1876, government in most Aboriginal communities has been based on laws in the Indian Act. These are laws made by the federal government.

One part of the Indian Act says that Aboriginal groups on reserves must elect a leader. In most Aboriginal cultures, though, the head of a group either inherited the position or was chosen after a group discussion. Voting wasn't the traditional way of doing things.

Today, Aboriginal groups want to make their own decisions on the best form of government for their communities. This might be traditional or modern, or a combination of both.

One exciting change was the creation of the territory of Nunavut on 1 April 1999. Newspapers and magazines all across Canada had information about this important event. You can learn more about it in the following report.

Today, many unfair laws have been changed. For example, all people are free to practise their beliefs, and there are no more residential schools

Nunavut Is Born

IQALUIT, 1 April 1999 Today the Inuit hopes for self-government came true when the territory of Nunavut was created. In Inuktitut, Nunavut means "our land."

The ceremonies to create Nunavut were held in Iqaluit, the capital of the new territory. The new legislature building was too small to hold all the guests, so people gathered in a large building at the airport.

Outside, fireworks lit the dark sky. Inside, there were speeches and drum dancing. A traditional soapstone lamp was lit as a symbol of strength. Three Elders watched over everything as papers were signed to create the territory.

The Inuit had been working for 30 years for this moment. The area that is now Nunavut used to be part of the Northwest Territories.

Most of the people in the area are Inuit. Inuit culture had trouble surviving after the arrival of Europeans. The Inuit in the eastern part of the Arctic believed they could do a better job of taking care of their own people.

Nunavut's first premier, Paul Okalik, said, "We, the people of Nunavut, have regained control of our destiny. Today we stand strong and welcome the challenges Nunavut faces."

Reported by Margaret Matthews

Just after midnight on Friday, 1 April 1999, fireworks lit the night sky over Iqaluit to celebrate the new territory of Nunavut

Nunavut Facts

Official languages: Inuktitut, English, and French
85% of the people speak Inuktitut

Size: 20% of Canada's land area
About the size of
British Columbia, Alberta, and Yukon together

Population: 25 000 people
By comparison,
the population of BC is 3 724 500

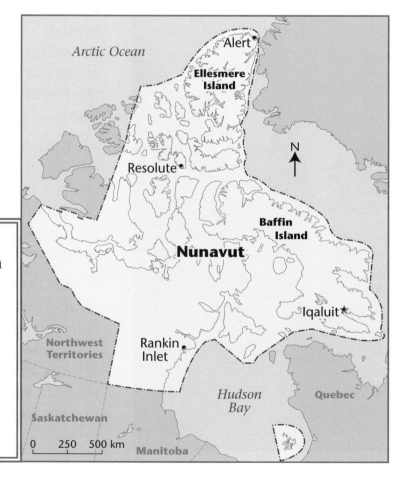

Paul Okalik displays a model of the new Nunavut coin made to mark the creation of the new territory.

Women wearing traditional caribou skins joined the celebrations in Nunavut.

How the New Government Will Work

In elections, the people of Nunavut will vote for MLAs in 19 ridings. Together, these MLAs will form the Legislative Assembly. The MLAs will then elect a premier to lead them.

The Legislative Assembly will meet in a round room designed with benches around the side. The benches are covered with seal-skin. The room's ceiling is shaped like the ceiling of an igloo.

Guests at the Nunavut celebrations tour the new legislative building in Iqaluit.

Try This

Compare the government of Nunavut to traditional Inuit government. Think about the ways in which decisions are made. You'll probably need to review Chapter 4 for information on what traditional Inuit government was like. How is the new government different from the traditional ways? In what ways does the new government respect the traditions of the past?

You have seen different types of comparison charts in this book. Choose one that you think would work to present this comparison. Or you might want to invent a new chart of your own.

Find Out

News events today become history in the future! Try to find out about issues that are important to Aboriginal peoples in your community today. You can find information in newspapers and on television and radio news programs. You might want to get information by interviewing people who are working to make a difference.

Lively Communities

Aboriginal people today are working in their communities to make sure young people learn their own languages and understand their history and culture. They are doing this in two ways. One way is by practising traditional ceremonies. The other way is by using old traditions to create new ones.

Passing on Names

In many Aboriginal cultures, names have a great importance. By keeping up the tradition of passing on ancestral names, people are keeping their past alive. They are also recording their rights to the land and its resources for the future.

Today, many Aboriginal people have two "first names." One is the name they go by in everyday life. The other is an ancestral name they are called on special occasions such as potlatches.

New Traditions

In the past, powwows were held by Plains peoples to celebrate something or to prepare for war against another group. Today, powwows are friendly social events where many different Aboriginal groups come together. They are a new tradition in many communities.

At powwows, people dance in a big circle called an **arbor**. The dances are a type of prayer honouring the creator of all life.

Is there something special your community is doing to keep your culture strong? How can you help?

Potlatches are an important way people in Kwakwa̱ka'wakw communities today keep the traditions of the past and pass on rights and honours to the next generation.

Tom Sampson

The Sampson family is from the Wsanec [wuh-SAN-ek] area of southern Vancouver Island in British Columbia. The Wsanec are one of the Straits Salish peoples.

Tom Sampson is the eldest of 12 children. Their father, Francis Wayne Sampson, was Wsanec, but their mother, Watanmay [WAH-tun-may], was Nez Perce. The Nez Perce are Plains peoples who are from what is now called Idaho in the United States. The history of Tom's family goes back thousands of years.

Here Tom explains how his family has worked to keep alive the traditions of the past. He also talks about how Canadian laws made it hard to keep up their family traditions.

The purpose of the powwow is to honour the person, the name, and the land and the spirituality that comes with it. We hold a powwow to honour our mother, to respect her, and to show that we are from her. We respect her side of the family as much as we respect our father's side.

We were told by our mother that we had to know our father's ways first. So we learned about our father's ways and got all the names in place. Then we could begin to practise our mother's ways.

It took us a long time to learn everything we needed to know about our father's ways. When the Europeans came in they destroyed or took our sacred belongings. Many things were burned. People tried to hide masks and never spoke about them for many generations. Europeans didn't like to see that we had masks and songs to sing because it wasn't part of their culture. When I was young it was illegal to practise our beliefs.

Today, we are strong again in our father's ways, so now we are looking to our mother's ways.

The powwow is also coming together to have fun and dance. We don't charge money for our powwow. Our teaching is that when you invite people, you don't ask them to pay to come into your house. You invite them and welcome them.

A Closer Look

A Powwow

This powwow took place on a summer weekend. People started arriving many days before. Some people set up tents to sell crafts and food. Others came to dance and drum.

The Sampson family and other people in the community worked hard for weeks to get everything ready. There was a stage for the announcer and places for people to sit to watch the dancing. They also put notices in newspapers and on the radio. They wanted to make sure everyone knew they were invited to come to the powwow.

During the powwow the family served food. The meal everyone looked forward to the most was smoked salmon and **bannock** [BAN-uk]. Bannock is a type of fried bread.

The Grand Entrance is one of the most exciting parts of the powwow. First come the flags and the eagle-feather standard, followed by the dancers in their **regalia** [rih-GALE-yuh]. The regalia are the special clothing worn for these celebrations. There are different styles of powwow dancing and different styles of regalia for each one.

This Grand Entrance took place on the afternoon when young people were dancing, so young people were chosen to carry the flags and the eagle-feather standard. The boy carrying the standard is Anastacio [an-az-TA-zeo] (Sonny) Garcia, Tom Sampson's great-nephew. The eagle feathers represent the many different groups that come together for a powwow. The boy in front is Sonny's friend Ian Sam.

The music for powwow dancing is made by drum groups. There is one large drum in the centre and several people who beat the drum. There is one lead singer, but the other people in the group also join in. The music has a strong rhythm and the singing is powerful. It makes you want to dance!

Sonny Garcia has done powwow dancing since he was seven years old. He says, "The thing I like about powwows is meeting so many different people from so many places. We get together with family from far away and make new friends."

Sonny is wearing his regalia for the grass dance. The grass dance was done by many Plains groups and had different meanings for each group. The name refers to the grass a warrior carried on his belt to start campfires.

Try This

In a group, discuss different ways people have of coming together to celebrate their culture and history.

On your own, select one of these ways of celebrating and compare it to a powwow. Describe one thing that is the same and one thing that is different.

What YOU Can Do!

In all cultures, every person has a chance to make a contribution. This includes you!

Some people are famous for their contributions. Others work quietly in their communities. How are the people in these photographs contributing to their communities? How would you like to contribute?

Honouring

In our communities we often do things to honour people who have made important contributions.

The contributions Aboriginal peoples have made to our country have not always been honoured by other Canadians. Today, many Canadians believe that it is important to change this.

One way to change this is to learn as much as you can about the contributions of Aboriginal peoples, past and present. Then, tell others what you know. This is one way you can make your own contribution to helping people get along!

Think For Yourself

Tom Sampson's family honours their mother with a powwow each year. How would you honour an Aboriginal person?

Pick an Aboriginal person to honour. You might choose from:
- a person in this book
- a person from the past or present that you have read about
- a person who is important in your life

Decide on a way to honour this person. You might make a small statue, a certificate, or a speech. You could work in a group to plan a celebration. Whatever you do, make it special!

The Totem Pole of Knowledge on the grounds of the Parliament Buildings in Victoria is one way the government of BC honours the contributions of Aboriginal peoples to Canada. This totem pole was carved by Cicero August of the Cowichan First Nation. It was erected in 1990. At the same time, a copy was erected in Auckland, New Zealand. These totem poles help link the people of the two countries.

Looking Back

In this chapter, you had a chance to think about the ways in which events in the past have affected what is happening today. You also saw how the things we do as individuals and the laws we make can change things for tomorrow.

Think back on what you have learned this year in social studies. What is the BIG IDEA that you most want to remember?

Index

Numbers in **boldface** indicate an illustration.

Photo Credits

p. 12 Archive Photos;

p. 21 First Light;

p. 26 Valan Photos;

p. 34 (t) Loralee Case,
(b) CORBIS/Sharna Balfour; ABPL;

p. 35 (t) Sharon Sterling, (b) CORBIS/Galen Rowell;

p. 38 CORBIS/Natalie Fobes;

p. 39 Image Network Inc.;

p. 41 British Columbia Archives/A-03579;

p. 43 Al Harvey;

p. 44 Image Network Inc.;

p. 45 Gary Fiegehen;

p. 51 CORBIS/© Kennan Ward;

p. 61 Reproduced by permission of the West Baffin Eskimo Co-operative Ltd.;

p. 63 First Light;

p. 78 Royal British Columbia Museum/1350;

p. 79 Royal BC Museum/PN7707-31;

p. 81 Glenbow Archives/NA 1406;

p. 83 Photograph courtesy of the Royal Ontario Museum, © ROM;

p. 85 Royal British Columbia Museum/4606;

p. 88 Royal BC Museum/PN 13492;

p. 91 Valan Photos;

p. 93 Image Network Inc.;

p. 98 Royal BC Museum/4489;

p. 103 Gary Fiegehen;

p. 106 CORBIS/Gary Braasch;

p. 108 Valan Photos;

p. 109 Royal BC Museum/CPN14076;

p. 110 (t) David Neel Photography,
(m) CORBIS/Hal Horwitz, (b) Valan Photos;

p. 111 (t) Courtesy Secwepemc Cultural Education Society, (b) BC Archives/B03802;

p. 118 CORBIS/Archivo Iconografico,S.A.;

p. 121 The Granger Collection, New York;

p. 123 John Cabot leaving Bristol, by Harold Goodridge, commissioned by the Newfoundland Historical Society in 1947, and reproduced courtesy of the Society and the present owners,
the Government of Newfoundland and Labrador. Photo by Ned Pratt;

p. 125 Evening Telegram – Joe Gibbons/Canapress;

p. 126 Valan Photos;

p. 132 Nova Scotia Museum/NSM 59.60.3;

p. 136 National Archives of Canada/C38862;

p. 137 Publiphoto;

p. 142 National Archives of Canada/C13938;

p. 147 National Archives of Canada/C11014;

p. 148 Image Network Inc.;

p. 149 Glenbow Archives/7-35;

p. 150 National Archives of Canada/C73448;

p. 153 (bl) Canadian Museum of Civilization/08589,
(tr) Newfoundland Museum, (br) Canadian Museum of Civilization/S814371;

p. 154 The Granger Collection, New York;

p. 158 Courtesy William Gould;

p. 160 National Archives of Canada/C6861;

p. 165 Manitoba Museum of Man and Nature. Artifacts from the Hudson's Bay Company Museum Collection;

p. 167 National Archives of Canada/C2774;

p. 168 Glenbow Archives/NA1406-4;

p. 170 Image Network Inc.;

p. 171 National Archives of Canada/C11201;

p. 174 Royal BC Museum/PN4608,

p. 175 Royal BC Museum/PN4881;

p. 176 Royal BC Museum/PN238;

p. 184 (t) Image Network Inc., (b) Destrube Photography;

p. 186 BC Archives/85097;

p. 188 Victoria Times Colonist – Ray Smith/Canapress;

p. 190 Kevin Frayer/Canapress;

p. 191 Kevin Frayer/Canapress;

p. 193 David Neel Photography;

p. 196 (l) Victoria Times Colonist – Debra Brash/Canapress;

p. 197 (t) Image Network Inc., (m) David Lucas/Canapress, (b) Halifax Daily News/Sandor Fizli/Canapress;

p. 198 Destrube Photography